SINGING WITH THE SIRENS

OVERCOMING THE

LONG-TERM EFFECTS

OF CHILDHOOD

SEXUAL EXPLOITATION

ELLYN ROBERTS BELL

STACEY AULT BELL

Published 2015
Printed in the United States of America
ISBN: 978-1-63152-936-8
Library of Congress Control Number: 2014922700

Interior design by Tabitha Lahr

For information, address:
She Writes Press
1563 Solano Ave #546
Berkeley, CA 94707

She Writes Press is a division of Spark Point Studio

DEDICATION

To Molly and Peter—children of my body, you have given me such joy since the days of my youth. I love you with fierceness.

—ERB

To the children I birthed—you saved my life. Everything I am and everything I do is because of your love. To all my other babies—unlike the others, I chose you and am eternally grateful for the light you shine. You are my Jesus with skin on.

—SAB

EPIGRAPH

Crashing forward, waves before me—
Do I ride them or do I drown?
How am I to trust the motion? I may falter and go down.
But in thrashing, arms about me,
Gasping, struggling for breath, I found
If I only let the water hold me.
Forceful rushing of salty presence
Carries me to holy ground.

CONTENTS

PROLOGUE

We smiled as we heard the voice resonating from her cell: a soft, soulful mourning filled with melody and pain. She sang of the mothers and fathers who had rejected her, the men who had abused her, the sisters who had mistreated her. She sang as though she thought nobody was listening and yet sang as though she were in front of an audience of millions. She sang for herself, she sang for God, she sang for us.

Just minutes before, she had described her song in a group of fifteen girls in a detention center's girls' group. She had shared hesitantly, as if she wasn't sure if it was time to tell her secret. She had shared although she seemed uneasy and unsure, somehow afraid that if she confided her gift, the imps of fate would take from her the only thing she had left.

The topic was "From where do you draw your strength?" We had been coming to the facility to spend time with girls who had been arrested, many of whom had been commercially sexually exploited or abused from a young age. We were there to give them an opportunity to find their voice. We went around the room.

"I get my strength from *mi familia*," said Ameliana, her crisp Mexican accent merry as she tossed her head back. Her eyes became serious. "They miss me," she said. "My little brothers and sisters, they don't understand what's going on."

"I get my strength from my culture," said Ly, a petite Hmong girl with full lips and high cheekbones.

"Tell us more about that," Ellyn said softly.

"You know . . . everything my parents went through, my ancestors went through, makes this shit here seem easy!"

The girls listened. A lot of them didn't have a frame of reference for parents, let alone ancestors. Like autumn leaves falling to the ground, they had no branches, no tree, no roots.

"My parents were in Thailand in a refugee camp when my sister and brothers were born. They came to the US with nothing." Ly stopped, already afraid she had said too much.

"I sing," said Shardae, her voice almost a whisper. We looked at her.

"Singing gives you strength?" Stacey asked, validating her statement, asking for more.

"I love to sing. It makes me feel free." She smiled ever so slightly. The corners of her mouth tilted upward as though she wanted to recall a memory, a time she had felt free. She lifted her hand to her hair and twirled it slowly. Her hair was short, curly, brown. The weave had been cut out when she got locked up. She didn't feel quite pretty enough without it. Her skin was the color of clay, its reddish tint indicating a multicultural heritage, partnerships between Africans and Native Americans long before she was born. Acne marks scarred her cheeks, reminding us all of the nervous habit she'd had of picking her face. Her eyes were as deep as the deepest well; they had seen too much, cried too many tears. She didn't cry much anymore. Her tears were internal, great sobs that tore at the inside of her heart—cries none of us heard. "I sang when I got arrested," she said, more loudly this time.

The girls laughed.

"That's hella funny!"

"What they say? They probably thought your ass was crazy!"

"Hell yeah . . . ha ha ha."

Shardae flinched, already annoyed she'd shared too much, still scared someone might take her gift if they knew where she hid it.

We glanced at each other. Observing the subtle change in her demeanor, Ellyn intervened. The girls, not yet as aware of one another, didn't notice.

"I feel a talent show coming on," said Ellyn, smiling. "Want to sing for us?"

"I wanna sing." The voices came now, alpha females, those who had worked their way to the top, wanting the spotlight. "We wanna rap."

We smiled; they were finding their voices. They were eager to be heard. Dying for someone to listen to them, watch them, touch them.

"It's Shardae's turn," Stacey said, meeting her gaze.

"Naw, I ain't finna sing now! I was singing then, though. The police was yelling, I was singing. The lights was flashing, I was singing. I knew my ass was coming back to this place; I was gonna sing all the way here. . . . I was singing with the sirens," she said loudly.

The group laughed again. The moment was over, but we understood. We could picture her in our minds, singing sweetly to herself as the sirens wailed around her, defiant that she had a gift of song and she wasn't going to give it away. They could lock her up, but they couldn't take her voice.

She wasn't going to sing for us today, at least not in group. But she had spoken. She had given us a glimpse into her soul, an idea of the strength that lay deep within her. We knew we could still connect, and encourage, and heal . . . and sing.

We would meet lots of girls—girls who had dealt with exploitation on many different levels, from formal prostitution rings to survival sex to taking the rap for a boyfriend they didn't want to snitch on. As we walked the road with them, slowly helping them find their way back from their abuse, we contemplated our own exploitation, the abuse we had endured at the hands of family members, teenage boyfriends and grown men. We recognized these girls had a chance—an opportunity to change their trajectory and experience something sacred and beautiful in their future. Or did they?

We spent late nights searching for answers. How, decades after our own abuses, is our society still poised to steal, kill, and destroy the innocence of young women? Decades after the strides made in the women's movement, how is it that women espousing sexual empowerment describe freedom as having the ability to take pole-dancing classes at their gym? Decades after the domestic violence movement peaked, how is it that teen-dating violence is raging and rampant in our schools? Additionally, why are there still not adequate services for our children on the street and in the "system"? And why are so many bright and strong women still trapped in abusive situations that steal their voice, their power, and their ability to love?

Singing with the Sirens was birthed out of these questions. Throughout this book, we will address all of these issues in a creative, poignant, historical, and relevant way, using our own exploitation as a backdrop. Readers will travel with us, and with the young people who have shared their stories with us, on a healing journey. Come with us; be introspective—you may find medicine for what ails you. You may find, as we did, sometimes just showing up for someone else puts your own life in perspective and gives you back the will to sing.

PART I

FROM WHERE WE CAME

CHAPTER I

THE SIREN

To know our history is to begin to see how to take up the struggle again.[1]

We huddled together on the cliffs above the sea, the wind stinging our faces and nearly blowing us into puddles of mud on the rain-drenched bluffs. But we squarely faced that magnificent Pacific, eyes stinging from the swirling, salty air, arms wrapped around each other's shoulders, coats blowing back behind us. Halfway through writing this book, we were back in the place where the siren had called to us two years before.

It was like magic, the way it all happened. Here we were, all at once feeling as if the sky had opened up to us and we had smooth-sailing waters ahead. That was only the beginning, though; in the months following, we spoke daily, wrote continually, channeled visions and dreams, and spent as much time

---

1. Barbara Ehrenreich and Deirdre English, *Witches, Midwives & Nurses* (New York: Feminist Press at the City University of New York, 1993), 4.

as possible together in Ellyn's apartment above the sea. The sounds of the waves and the wind lulled us to sleep nightly. The sirens called to us, and we wrote the stories we knew—our stories, the stories of countless girls and women, and the stories of the misunderstood sirens.

We knew we had to write about the complexities of how a female soul gets lost when she is not valued as a child or a young woman or if she is valued for the wrong reasons. We had seen too much, and we had to move through it all: the broken spirit that does not see its worth, the child who pleases others sexually at her own expense until there is no self left to give, the girls who never had a chance, and the ones who become lost women learning to hide and numb the old pain in various compensatory ways. We had worked with girls for years, we had worked with ourselves even longer, and we knew we could no longer remain silent. Our friendship gave us the courage, the will, and the confidence to write what we knew to be true, to write the truth of hidden and forgotten lives. And so we embarked upon this expedition together, finding the way along craggy cliffs and deep seawaters, and exploring with curiosity and grace how someone loses herself and then reclaims herself, piece by piece, until she finds some semblance of wholeness.

Time has passed now, as it always does. We finished writing the first draft of this book during the last days of 2012 and the day before Ellyn's adoptive mother died. Then, as we both got busy doing other things, our sense of direction faded into the dim light of inertia and uncertainty about how to proceed. Stacey was actively involved in a doctoral program, working full-time for a large urban school district, and caring for her

kids. Ellyn had taken a position in San Francisco and was ending political ties in Sacramento. We forgot in a way how to
proceed, if we ever really knew. But that is part of the healing
process, too: we overcome the obstacles that stand in our way,
and we keep moving forward.

Although both young females and young males are abused
and exploited, and both suffer the consequences to the body
and the psyche, this book focuses on sexual exploitation of
females specifically and its consequences for women's adulthood. Unlike many memoirists, we are not writing merely to
tell *our* story—we are writing to tell *a* story, one that applies
to many women and girls who may never be seen or known,
but whose pain and struggles are real. We write for them, for
our daughters and their daughters, and for the little girls who
have touched our hearts along the way. This is the reason why
we do not identify by actual name the subjects of the stories,
and why we use anonymous first and third-person narrative
throughout many of them.

It is the essence and commonality of our collective pain,
the long, spiral journeys, and the capacity for healing that we
want to get across to readers. Through our work, we have experienced firsthand the residual effects of sexual trauma at an
early age and have acquired insights into how to live in a way
that is true to our souls, despite it all. We are just two women
of millions who know this tale too well.

This book is a healing narrative, a medicine book, prescrip-
tive nonfiction, and a quest. This is a book for any woman who
has suffered because of sexual, mental, emotional, or physical
abuse or violence, especially those whose pain began in child-

hood. It is also for the girls and women who have landed in the middle of the sex industry, unsure of where their value derives from, after years of sexual trauma. It is about finding the power within and the will to heal that embraces all shame and transforms it into power and grace.

The siren is not a seductress of men, a vision of a patriarchal fantasy, or a product from Victoria's Secret. She is the strong and unrelenting heroine of a female life. She seeks to be found and to be known, and she calls to us all to wake up to true power in this world—the transformative abilities we all hold within us. What does it mean to become the heroine of your life? Let these stories and this journey help you tell your own story and find your way to wholeness as you define it.

We give thanks for the sirens who would not let us remain silent and urged us to sing.

The story of the siren is ancient, complex, and difficult to discern fully. Superstition and folklore give us incomplete tales. Sirens in Greek mythology were companions of Persephone before Hades raped her and took her to the underworld. Her mother, the goddess Demeter, searched relentlessly for Persephone and enlisted the sirens to assist her in that search. In some accounts, the sirens were maidens with birdlike bodies from the waist down. They grew wings in order to fly and find Persephone. They played musical instruments and were said to have had beautiful and haunting voices.

Sirens also factor prominently in the epic poem *The Odys-*

sey, as the magical seawomen of Sirenum Scopuli, three small islands off the coast of Capri, who caused ships to wreck on their rocky shores by compelling the sailors to destruction with their mesmerizing songs. *The Odyssey*—written circa 630 BCE and attributed to Homer (though some speculate that it was actually by an unknown woman)—recounts the story of Ulysses, or Odysseus, and his men on a return voyage from Troy to their home in Ithaca. Theirs is an adventure of land and sea, as well as of body and spirit. In Book Twelve of *The Odyssey*, their ship encounters the Island of the Sirens, and Ulysses instructs his men to fill their ears with wax to avoid hearing the voices of the sirens and being brought to doom by their sweet singing. Although the crew plugs their ears, Ulysses instructs them to bind him to the mast of the ship, with his ears unplugged, in order to hear and yet avoid and steer past the powerful temptation. The ship holds its course as the music grows fainter and then ceases to be audible, and thus the crew narrowly escapes the fate of being lost, crazed, and imminently dead.

The early Christians carried on the tradition of fearing the sirens. In the fourth century, Vulgate, the Latin translation of the Christian Bible attributed to Saint Jerome, mentions of "sirens" in Isaiah 13:

And that Babylon, glorious among kingdoms, the famous pride of the Chaldeans, shall be even as the Lord destroyed Sodom and Gomorrha. It shall no more be inhabited for ever, and it shall not be founded unto generation and generation: neither shall the Arabian pitch his tents there, nor shall the shepherds rest there. But wild beasts shall rest

*there, and their houses shall be filled with serpents, and
ostriches shall dwell there, and the hairy ones shall dance
there. And owls shall answer one another there, in the
houses thereof, and sirens in the temples of pleasure.*[2]

Early Christian fathers, who propagated much of today's
lingering patriarchal thought, may have interpreted this instance of "siren" as a metaphor for worldly temptations of the
flesh and thus often used sirens as symbols of the inherent danger that women embodied.

Sirens in modern-day popular culture are often viewed as
synonymous with mermaids, although sirens are sometimes
described as hateful and dangerous, while mermaids are perceived as more passive, beautiful, and pure. In fact, the word
"mermaid" literally means "virgin of the sea," in diametrical
opposition with the luring, sensual, destructive, and soulful
calling of the historical siren. It is not surprising that the theme
of woman as pure virgin or temptress/whore appears even in
these long-ago tales of mermaids and sirens—the boundaries and limits restricting women with their many tentacles are
deeply connected to such stories and myths that we live out in
our everyday lives, both historic and current.

But this is not the full story.

The sea holds the mysteries of human existence and
our beginnings as a species. In the book *The Great Cosmic
Mother*, Monica Sjöö and Barbara Mor do an excellent job of
documenting our origins in this regard. They conclude, as did
Charles Darwin, that the female principle is the primordial ele-
ment of the sea, and that "in the beginning, life did not gestate

---

2. Isaias 13: 19–22, http://latinvulgate.com.

within the body of any creature, but within the ocean womb containing all organic life."[3] As a matter of course, this is not a "history" to which we are generally exposed, so like many other evolutionary stories of gender and sexuality, the information remains inaccessible unless you are looking for it. Further, within all of the available knowledge about female sexuality, the dominant powers of our world still have a need to control the conversation and the information. If we rewrote the stories of creation and sexuality, stories of how we all came to be here, then we would have to face facts about the exploitation of women and children, as well as the exploitation of the earth, differently. If we truly were to look at the information that makes good sense, rather than the carefully selected, dominant creation story that disempowers women for all time, then we would begin to understand our amazing, original nature and not be bound by shackles that threaten to destroy us before we are ever born into this life.

As we begin to explore this corruption of female sexuality and the pain it has caused, we also seek vindication for those whose lives have been forgotten or made invisible. It's like a thread that one pulls on, and soon the sweater falls apart—you can't begin to address this issue solidly, and with the necessary integrity for change, unless you pull that thread.

As we have lived, and by finding voice among the following pages, we are pulling on the thread. In doing so, we are also following the call of the siren, and instead of destruction, temptation, or vice, we are finding redemption. We have dreamed of her, smelled her salty breath, felt her in our own skin. We have come to understand the siren in a new way that embodies

---

3. Monica Sjöo and Barbara Mor, *The Great Cosmic Mother* (San Francisco, HarperCollins, 1991).

an ancient, lived experience of women—not one of revisionist lust and temptation, but one of strength, grace, air, and water, wings and fish tails, one that beckons us to reclaim and reinvent our own stories and find the base of our longing and belonging.

We collectively have the ability to create a new story, one that does not define our sexuality by the standards of the dominant culture but rather embraces it as part of a deeper, more intrinsic power that we carry in our souls. This new story celebrates our femaleness, our fierceness, and life itself, in all its cyclical and beautiful stages, and helps us not to be hurt, minimized, objectified, or used by another. In these pages, we put forth the rallying cry to speak the shame that has silenced so many, and to transform that silence and pain into words, myth, art, and song.

We understand the siren as a symbol of the divine feminine; of the power of the ocean; of the need to heal our personal lives, our society, and this planet; and, most importantly, of how all these things are interconnected. We believe that our very survival depends upon this healing.

Long ago, when the world was newer than it is today and more people believed in the gods and goddesses of nature, magic was witnessed often and no one questioned its validity. In those times, it was not uncommon for the people who dwelled near the sea to hear of strange happenings and circumstances. Mostly the creatures who appeared during these events remained a mystery, relegated to late-night talks over ale, but on rare occasions, they made themselves known. One of these times was in a tiny village just south of Galway. A beautiful and happy young girl, a maiden, was taken by some drunken young men who disdained her freedom. The men used her and hurt her and left her naked and alone by an abandoned farmhouse. After making her way back to the village, she was greeted with the silence of her mother and the coldness of her father. Her family turned their backs on her in disgust. The parish priest called her a harlot and wounded her where she stood.

As her shame grew, she hid herself away. When she found her body changing and realized that she was with child, she stowed away on a boat to the Aran Islands, hiding under a blanket, stifling her tears, and burying her pain deep within. She felt alone in the world. The women of the sea knew this and watched silently, swimming in fishlike form alongside the boat, unknown to the girl.

Once night fell and the boat and the docks had emptied into the nearby tavern, she walked to the cliffs above the sea. She felt hungry and thirsty, but there was no one to provide food, drink, or warmth. It took her some time to walk the path in the darkness, but she found the highest cliff possible, and at daybreak she tossed herself into the water below. Expecting death and oblivion, she was surprised to find life as the bird women caught her in their net in midair and carried her to their sisters in the water, where she took on her new form—part fish, part woman, and at times part bird.

"The Mother Goddess won't let you drown," they said. "You have a new body and a new life; you are beautiful, and you are one of us now." And so she was.

As time passed, fishermen near Galway said they had seen a phantom of the girl who had disappeared from the village, or had gotten a fleeting glimpse of her face on a sea creature's body. Some of their boats were strangely overturned and hurled onto the rocks in storms over the next few seasons, and several men disappeared. Once, a tall woman in a dark cape appeared on the rocks, her arms outstretched as if commanding the wind—perhaps she was the Morrígan, an Irish mother goddess, or one of a trio of goddesses, who appears as both woman and bird—for once spotted she was gone, and a crow remained in her place.

There were many stories told over the generations. But the lessons were never learned.

In our work with young women, as well as with adult women, we hear the common theme of puritan versus whore. Although sexual, it is also symbolically larger than sexuality and related to the very worth of an individual. The "whore" is the one who is cast aside and sometimes even labeled as less than human—as in the cases of murdered prostitutes whose files state there was "no human involved."[4] Young women all over the globe go from being innocent children to being sacrificed for adult male pleasure through no fault of their own. Furthermore, the act of using a child in this way and then faulting the child for the actions of the adult is common in child sexual abuse and exploitation.

---

4. Reported to be a common slang police term used for when a prostitute is murdered. Radicalreference.info states: "In 'NHI-No Humans Involved,' UCSD faculty member Elizabeth Sisco traces the use of the term to the San Diego area during the 1980s and 1990s, by San Diego police, to address a series of murders and sexual assaults against women. Sisco wrote that the head of the task force assigned to investigate the murders claimed that the use of 'NHI' is fictionalized by old detective novels, but another San Diego officer confirmed the use of the 'NHI' term in a *Sacramento Bee* article to describe these murders."

Even if many women are largely silent about the effects of their abuse, today we encounter more open information about child trafficking and sexual exploitation—commercial, familial, and for survival. Part of this upsurge in information is related to the Internet and the ways in which it is linked to the sexual exploitation of minors, as well as the easy access it offers to pornography and sexually violent images. Also, as happens within a culture, we become desensitized to something awful and then require something even more awful to awaken that same feeling of horror.

Twenty years ago, we as a society were concerned and shocked by homelessness and the plight of people living on the streets. Now, we think of homelessness as common and we barely notice when a homeless person passes by us. Similarly, the pornography that Andrea Dworkin wrote about in the 1970s and '80s would barely offend today's sensibilities. Our appetites for pornography have grown more violent and degrading as people become more accustomed to the effects of violence and explicit sex acts.

In addition, forty years ago, sexual assault and domestic violence were new topics of concern for the general public. In 1976, there was not even one battered-women's shelter in New York City. The violence women suffered in their own homes was literally invisible to most of the population. Social service and religious organizations provided assistance to women in need, but a larger-scale acknowledgment of violence against women did not exist. By 1981, there were five battered-women's shelters in New York City, and all were filled to capacity and forced to turn away eighty-five of every one hundred women requesting services.[5]

---

5. Susan Schechter, *Women and Male Violence* (Boston: South End Press, 1982).

As previously unmentioned acts of violence toward wives and girlfriends began to be spoken about, well-intentioned groups and individuals came forward to assist in various ways. Now, domestic violence shelters and sexual-assault centers are institutionalized and found in most counties or larger communities throughout the United States.

The shelter movement was driven by a need to expose the violence that many women were experiencing in their lives. Women who are physically abused are often subject to other forms of abuse as well, including rape and verbal assault. Many mental health professionals of the late 1970s and early '80s blamed women for the abuse that they suffered and searched for evidence of some kind of character flaw in those victims. Fortunately, in the early 1980s, a group of formerly battered women in Duluth, Minnesota and their advocates developed the "power and control wheel," which assisted them to interpret the abuse that they had endured. This framework was readily understood by women who had experienced similar violence. By the mid- to late 1980s, almost all dominant theories on domestic violence pointed back to the issue of power and control exercised by perpetrators of violence or abuse.

The power and control wheel has been translated into numerous languages over the years and adapted for other social issues in which one person uses his or her power and privilege as a means of gaining control over another person or person(s).[6] The core of the wheel is the need for power and dominance, and the spokes of the wheel are the ways in which this power is kept alive as a threat. The outside of the wheel is physical violence or survival threats that keep the "victim" from escaping or being able to leave.

---

6. The Duluth Model, Domestic Abuse Intervention Programs, http://duluthmodel.org./powerandcontrol.pdf.

Despite all of our advances over the years, we are still observing the rise of violence against women and the normalization and increase of sexual assault through rape culture. The issue underlying domestic violence, rape, trafficking, and prostitution is a shared one—a deep, strong undercurrent of belief that some people are inherently more valuable than others and that some, often young women, are disposable, replaceable objects. It has never been about sex; it is about who holds the power and how they wield and use that power in relation to another. The real rallying cry of the feminist and domestic violence movements was that women were autonomous individuals with value, undeserving of denigration and abuse. Yet women are still living in a world where value is assigned by class, skin color, sex, gender, age, and sexual orientation; this is the gnarly root that binds these issues together and that informs us that if we do not address the reasons behind our latest hot topic or societal cause, then we will not be able to make a true difference in the lives of those who have been affected.

We must also awaken to the connections between our disdain of and simultaneous participation in these systems that keep us and others in bondage. Addressing the issue will require looking at how individuals can make change and how, by waking ourselves up to what exists around us, we can then breathe life into a movement toward creating whole human beings who stand with one another, naming atrocities and helping others to do the same. It has never been about "rescuing" or "fixing broken women"; it is about building strength, resilience, community, and empathy with those who have been oppressed. It is about seeing our faces in their faces and knowing that those faces are the same.

Federal law describes the crime of child sex trafficking as the "recruitment, harboring, transportation, provision, or obtaining of a person for the purpose of a commercial sex act." [7] These acts include, but are not limited to, the exploitation of children through prostitution, pornography, and/or stripping. In the context of our work with both minor victims and adult survivors, we define sexual exploitation more globally, to include sexual molestation, sexual assault, and acquaintance or date rape. Equally devastating are the effects felt by young people engaging in survival sex (sex for food, clothing, a place to stay, etc.).

Those of us working with teens and young women have addressed these issues for years. However, the recent surge in commercial sexual exploitation, especially through prostitution, has placed agencies and practitioners on high alert and caused people to question the systems that remain in place in the United States and that set the stage for such heinous violence and widespread exploitation of children. As we address childhood sexual exploitation, we should not consider it the new cause of the day, where men lurk in the shadows of shopping malls, waiting to snatch our children. Instead, we should look at the systemic constructs, both historical and modern, that have popularized the so-called "oldest profession in the world"—not in the red-light districts of London, Amsterdam, and New York, but in the motels of our cities both big and small, in the hallways of our schools, and in the homes and lives of our most marginalized young people. We should con-

---

7. Child Welfare Council of California, "Ending the Commercial Exploitation of Children: A Call for Multi-System Collaboration in California", (December 7, 2012), 11.

sider how we view young women as sirens—not as those who lure men to destruction, but as women who, as a result of of the exploitation in their own young lives, become destined to a devastation of their own unless we provide them with opportunities to heal and create change. We should consider our role, as community members and leaders, as we address the systems of oppression and exploitation that ensure perpetrators will always have access to someone broken enough to become a casualty of manipulation. We should also consider our role not as saviors sent to rescue victims and to impose on them condescending practices of redemption, but as partners with those oppressed by exploitation.

The following story is told from the viewpoint of a woman who experienced the pain of early sexual abuse, coupled with the power of words to cause damage.

"*Slut.*" The word projected out of her mother's mouth and landed on her face like spittle. The impact of the accusation sent her reeling backward. It hurt more than the slap that had landed on her cheek seconds earlier. Her face, still red from the hand that had struck her, would soon return to its smooth shade of honey brown, but her heart would take longer to heal. Would it ever be repaired? she wondered silently in the time that followed—seconds that seemed like hours.

Quickly, she recalled another time she had heard that word. This recent denunciation seemed to have tapped an old wound, like a knife bearing down on unhealed flesh. She didn't feel like a "slut," yet she didn't quite know what one should feel like. She ascertained there must be truth to the accusation—after all, she was pregnant, she was a child, she wasn't married.

She grabbed her belly and turned away from the curse, from the yelling, from the anger. She walked to the bathroom, glad she hadn't retaliated, glad she hadn't spat back venomous words, glad she hadn't resorted to violence. She still had her dignity, and she made a decision now: she would maintain that for her child. It might be all she had, especially if she was a slut; did sluts have dignity?

Closing the bathroom door, she leaned back and closed her tear-filled eyes. It came back so fast. She was about thirteen, on a camping trip, at a hippie festival with her family. She ended up intoxicated and half-clothed in the tent of a boy, or maybe it was a man—she couldn't recall. She wasn't alone; another girl, a friend of the family, was with her, with the boy/man. They'd met him while dancing to some folk melody and giggled at his attention, felt pretty as the boy/man admired their eyes, their smiles, their shapes. They'd danced for him at first, swirling woozily, spinning, stretching.

She couldn't recall how they'd ended up in his tent, or half-naked, for that matter, but she remembered that she'd been discovered, and she remembered that word. . . .

"You *slut*!" Her stepmother had hurled it at her, cutting into her flesh with her words.

"Wait . . . what? . . . I didn't . . ." She tried to explain herself.

"I can't believe you, fuckin' slut."

She was confused. She was thirteen. Drunk. Unsupervised. He wanted her, came on to her, encouraged her. She didn't quite understand, yet one thing was apparent: She was a slut. It was her fault. Her stepmother was usually the feminist rock she relied on for suffragette-style support, yet now she pierced the girl's heart with her anger.

But wait—there was more. Even that wasn't the first time she'd heard it. The wound was older still.

She put the toilet seat down and sat slowly. Closing her eyes, she remembered—though she had actually never forgotten.

"You like it, don't you?" he giggled, masturbating over her, his hand between her legs. She didn't like it. It hurt. His fingers inside her felt like a thousand needles stabbing at her privates. She didn't squirm, though. Like a good little girl, she lay very still, motionless, even, waiting until it stopped and she could curl up and forget.

"You like it, don't you, you little slut?" He smiled. Her grandfather.

What's a slut? she remembered having thought as she danced on the ceiling, watching her motionless body. *I wonder if a slut is pretty. Is a slut smart? Does she like this?*

Tears fell from her eyes and spilled onto her cheeks. She stood up and looked into the bathroom mirror. The pain was dissipating; now she was pissed. When she had heard the word "slut" at school or from guys, she had always dismissed it angrily. "Fuck off," she'd say when they'd yell at her as she walked by. "You want it!" Then she'd laugh. But these wounds, these scars, were deeper. She had been called a slut since she was five years old. Since before she understood what it meant. The word "slut" had become her, and she had become it—a self-fulfilling prophecy, spoken into existence when she was just a little girl.

It would be years before she found the power and voice to admit the damage that had been done, and it would be years before she had the strength to do the work to overcome the power of that word. Recovering was a difficult and painstaking journey. She remembered being at the park with her little sister, yelling protectively at those bullies who threw out spiteful denunciations, "Sticks and stones can break my bones, but names can never harm me!"

She knew now, looking into that mirror, reliving the pain of a lifetime of words, that the proverb taught to millions of children all over the world was a lie. Sticks and stones could break your bones, but names could break your soul.

Water is the first of the elements, the mother of all things, according to the philosophers of the ancient Greek city Miletus.[8] It is from the murky depths of water that many creation myths, even in the Judaic and Christian traditions, emerge, and it is from water (a feminine principle) and the spirit (a masculine principle) that the rite of baptism in the Christian New Testament comes. Some say the baptismal font was once called the "womb of Mary," and it is no coincidence that the names of all the ancient sea goddesses relate back to the name Mary.[9] And as Sjöö and Mor state in *The Great Cosmic Mother*: "For two and a half billion years on Earth, all life-forms floated in the womb-like environment of the planetary ocean."[10]

Somewhere submerged in the depths of our history is a sto-

8. Barbara Walker, *The Women's Encyclopedia of Myths and Secrets* (San Francisco: Harper, 1983), 1066.
9. Ibid., 1066.
10. Sjöö and Mor, 2.

ry of how the mythological goddesses of the sea became dangerous sirens or beautiful mermaids. Somewhere in the history of modernity, we have taken the sensuality, the strength, the power, the many faces of woman and goddess and buried them in the sea of forgetfulness. Over time, through our religions and cultural shifts, we have demonized the mutuality and neutrality of the sea-goddess story, turning it into the myths of the whore, the slut, and the little girl who "wants it" just because she is cute and someone wants to partake in his or her satisfaction at her expense. We have turned the mother of all things into a dangerous, submerged, provocative siren.

The process of healing these deep wounds of oppression and sexual exploitation will begin only when we as a culture are ready to peel back the veil from our eyes and see how the very belief systems that we have held dear have kept us in bondage. On a personal level, we must become very brave, unflinching and true to ourselves, as we decide to face the journey to wholeness and pull the thread. Facing the religious, philosophical, and societal constraints that have called into question women's intrinsic value requires great personal fortitude. How do we find our way out? The siren has appeared and made herself known as our guide.

CHAPTER 2

LOSING THE VOICE

I learned to be silent before I could speak, and when I could speak, my need for silence was confirmed. I wanted to sing, but they laughed at me, so I did not. At first the voice was stolen, but later I gave it away.

Giving up the voice is synonymous with giving up personal power. It happens when one gives way to another, believing that the other's opinion, voice, authority, knowledge, importance, or worthiness exceeds one's own. Inherent self-doubt accompanies this act of giving up one's voice, and although it happens to all of us throughout our lifetimes in various times and circumstances, it seems to be especially prevalent in people whose deep inner voice was stifled or negated at an early age.

When the senses are shut down during childhood, because the basic goodness and innate common sense of the mind are incongruent with the experiences and lived realities of a young person, then the lived experience and the deeper knowledge of the soul collide. The child learns that what is known internally cannot be trusted, because the outside world denies the validity of this inner knowledge and life. When this occurs, a dissonance within the self becomes the known reality. Unfortunately, both the inner and the outer life suffer, because then neither can be trusted. Consequently, the deep inner voice becomes silent and doubts all that it believes to be true. The voice is thus hidden or lost and needs to be uncovered and found in order to be restored. Conversely, when a child is reared in such a way that caretakers, teachers, and parents nurture, value, and acknowledge her inner world, then she learns to speak out, hold personal power, and believe in herself.

Our relationships with power are complicated and unconsciously dictated by the society and the world that we live in. We are all the time dealing with dynamics of power in all of our relationships, but we don't necessarily verbalize or acknowledge how that power manifests itself.

Starhawk, a writer and leader in feminist spirituality, describes three types of power in her book *Truth or Dare: Encounters with Power, Authority, and Mystery*—"power-over, power-from-within, and power-with"—and notes that each aspect of power speaks its own language and is defined by its own mythology.[11] The "power-over" realm is defined by a worldview in which "value must be earned or granted," fear is the primary motivator, and hope is offered through obedience and compliance. This is the primary worldview, and its rigidity manifests itself in an internalized insecurity about our own worth and right to be in this world; it "drives us to compete for the tokens of pseudo-value." Worth is defined, evaluated, and rated

---

11. Starhawk, *Truth or Dare: Encounters with Power, Authority, and Mystery* (San Francisco: HarperCollins, 1987), 8–10.

against others in our school systems and workplaces, and by our mates, lovers and families. Power-over is the type of power that squelches the voice and that is often exhibited in abusive relationships, whether these relationships are with parental figures or intimate partners. For the sexually abused or exploited child, power-over is the dominant paradigm of day-to-day function.

Starhawk defines power-from-within as a radically different way of looking at and interacting with the world—from a place where all things and beings have inherent value, and value is not dictated by outside sources. Power-from-within is the language of poetry, metaphor, myth, and mystery—the language of the mystics, of changing consciousness and creating connections with a world far too complex to be defined and boxed in by easy definitions.

Power-with sees the world through relationships and values people based on "how they affect others and according to a history based on experience."[12] Power-with is the language of creating community, valuing social order through creative processes, and working together toward agreed-upon outcomes.

When we talk about the experience of "losing the voice" or silencing the deeper self, we are really talking about how the self has lost touch with its own internal worth and power-from-within. This experience of silencing is defined not by a onetime incident, but rather by a series of repeated experiences that gradually erode one's inherent sense of worth and trust in one's own deeper moral compass or understanding. How this happens is unique to each individual who experiences this loss, but the results are largely similar in that they manifest in a way that negates and neglects one's own value. That initial lack of

12. Ibid.

trust within oneself, coupled with the attendant self-doubt, allows the door to be opened to exploitation of all kinds. Youth who have these doubts will silence themselves and may begin to exhibit patterns of self-hate, depression, and anxiety, as well as other symptoms of disconnection or dissociation from themselves.

Adult women who were silent about abuse as children may find it difficult to reconnect with their deeper voice because so much of their life has been defined by others. To that extent, a woman might have internalized those external negating voices to the point where she cannot hear the deeper voice of worth and wisdom within herself at all. The lost voice may be exhibited in numerous ways in adult women, including depression, anxiety, and addictions, as well as a host of compensating behaviors to cover internal shame and pain. Feeling and dealing with this old, deep internal pain as an adult is a true challenge. The core issue is the person's belief that she is defective and unworthy of love, and that therefore her voice means nothing. As one adult woman survivor asked, "How does this pain not feel fatal?"

Curiously, and as we've noticed from our own experiences, even after years of work on becoming aware and cultivating that power-from-within, something like an abusive relationship, a heartbreak, a job loss, or a perceived failure of any kind can immediately throw a person backward into old patterns of self-doubt and despair. As insidious, deep-rooted, and nebulous as this problem can be, the silencing of the deeper self cannot be minimized or wished away; rather, it must be dealt with head-on.

The following story demonstrates how the voice is stolen from children and highlights the consequences that plague a child when she is not heard or encouraged to speak her truth.

~°~

The schoolroom was warm and brightly lit. The children sat at wooden desks, pencils sharpened and paper ready to complete the first task of the morning. The morning routine was familiar: the children were writing in their diaries. The older ones wrote about current events and other significant stories; the little ones wrote innocent depictions of their weekend at the beach or trip into town.

In order to get help with the difficult terms, the children toted their spelling books up to the teacher's desk and lined up. She would spell out the hard words, and the kids would go back to their desks and laboriously copy her perfect prose, determined to write as neatly and thoughtfully as possible.

It was hard to tell if the girl had thought much about her journal entry. Had she lain awake at night, wondering if today was a good time to tell? Or had she spontaneously taken her place in line to get help with her spelling, naive to the implication of her story? It didn't really matter. Was the clock ticking loudly? Were the children chattering about their stories? Could anyone hear her as she cleared her throat to ask her teacher for assistance?

"Miss?"

"Yes, dear." The teacher smiled. There was trust in her eyes, a sincerity that radiated her being.

"How do you spell 'safety pin'?" The words fell out of the child's mouth. She had her spelling book and pencil ready and confidently handed it to Miss. Surely Miss had the answer. Surely Miss could help.

"'Safety pin'? What are you trying to say, dear?" Miss smiled some more. The child watched Miss carefully. She assessed the situation and didn't feel fear, didn't sense danger. The teacher was smiling. The child was a smart girl. She always wrote the best stories. Everything was going to be fine.

"Um, 'safety pin.'" She cleared her throat. "I'm going to say, 'He put the safety pin in my bum.'"

The air left the room. The child knew. Something was very wrong. She shouldn't have asked. The clock was definitely ticking loudly now. The child knew how to focus on it. She heard the *tick-tock* and tried very carefully to slow her heart rate down so it kept the beat: *tick-tock, tick-tock.* She looked around. The other children were still chattering mostly to themselves, their heads down. They licked their pencils and carefully recorded their diary entries, transcribing the difficult words letter by letter. The child looked back at Miss.

"Bum!" Miss frowned. "That is not appropriate, is it?"

"Um, no, Miss."

"We don't speak or write such things, do we?"

"No, Miss."

"Now, go and start over, young lady. I expect you to write about something appropriate—something that happened this weekend that you can write in your notebook without being vulgar. Do you understand?"

She understood. You didn't speak of such things, especially

in school. Words like "bum" were inappropriate and shouldn't be discussed. Even though his fingers felt like safety pins forcing their way into the girl's vagina, Miss didn't want to hear or read such stories. Even at five, the girl knew she couldn't have asked Miss to spell "vagina." That was surely a bad word. She had thought "bum" would be mild enough for Miss. Even at five, she worried about her audience, censored her words to make them more palatable and easier to digest.

Mostly she just wanted someone to listen. She wanted to talk about it—no, she actually wanted to write about it. Hoped she would be able to put her thoughts into words and have them read by someone who would understand. She didn't hope to be rescued, didn't really know that was an option. She just wanted someone to read her heart.

A strange thing happens when someone finally plucks up enough courage to speak and is still not heard. The voice recedes. It withdraws to a safe place deep inside. It becomes a whisper drowned out by the chatter of others. It becomes secondary to the *tick-tock* of daily life. It becomes barely audible, even to the owner of the voice. It fades into the recesses of the heart and takes the self with it. Until it learns to speak, however, the self cannot truly be free. The words have to be spoken, the truth has to be told, whether in prose or poetry, dance or rap, to one person or millions. The voice must return.

The worst thing about losing the voice is that at some point, after years of being silenced by others, the self learns to become the harshest jailer of the voice. No one has to remind you that you that your thoughts or feelings don't matter. In fact, people can tell you that you *do* matter, that you are loved, and you may accomplish many things outwardly, but inside there is a part of the self that doubts and judges. It accepts fear as "just the way it is," believes that there is some flaw in the self, and grows accustomed to the discomfort.

As Starhawk notes in *Truth or Dare*, people are survivors of the weapons that our culture has used against the self. This phenomenon is apparent in women who repeat patterns of choosing unhealthy partners and lovers, who engage in self-abnegation and sacrifice for partners who don't care about them, and who no longer care for themselves. The voice may have been lost years ago, but the continued silence becomes deadly, and over the years it becomes a buried poison in the body and soul and leads ultimately to destruction of the self. How many women who have committed suicide have intentionally or unintentionally kept their years of pain and rage hidden and silently buried away from others and even themselves?

The loss of voice hurts us all in one way or another. We lose mothers, sisters, grandmothers, and friends to an unspeakable foe that lies within.

Abby was a woman who did not see her worth, and out of fear, she learned to keep her voice silent. She experienced sexual abuse as a young teenager through an act of rape and then the aftermath of being passed around by a series of men, including adult men, who didn't bother to see—or care—that she was crying when they fucked her. She didn't connect to the family that raised her. They were family in name only; they were not involved in her life or her thoughts. In fact, they did not notice that the fourteen-year-old girl was cutting herself with scissors and biting her hand until it bled at night. They were too busy with their own lives and problems to see her, and so she never told them anything about herself. When she tried, they did not listen. She was pretty and had an air of vulnerability at the same time. Everybody at her school had called her a slut and a whore before any of it began, so she figured they knew something that she did not. No one ever refuted it. She didn't know why, but within a year, she began to live up to their insults.

She began stealing and selling drugs for an adult man who said he loved her. He was nice and sometimes took her to the airport, telling her that one day they would leave this place together. He would take her far away and give her all that she wanted. It made her feel hopeful and free. He was married, but he said he loved her best and would leave his stupid, nagging wife. He didn't, though. The wife came after the girl, and he did not protect the girl from the abuse and threats. After he left, she lost all protection, and herself, too, in a maze of promiscuity and drugs. Drugs numbed the feelings and took them away. Sex connected her to other living beings—in hopes of connection and love—and then, after that failed, to power. She learned: *use them before they use you up*. She stole mean girls' boyfriends just for the fun of it. She stole from the boys. She stole from the girls. She fucked anyone she pleased or who had something she could gain. She hated herself, hated the boys; she hated them all.

Somehow, somewhere along the line, it became clear to her that she was going to kill herself and that this was exactly what people expected to happen. Many secretly and not so secretly wanted her to fail, or at least believed that she would fail. Failure seemed imminent and easy; figuring a way out was a much harder task. But through some blessed resilience within her conflicted mind, she chose the narrow road out of hell. It was never easy, and the process went back and forth for years. It wasn't as if she could "think" her way out of the situation; it was more like feeling along a dark wall until she saw a light in the distance. She kept moving, though. Some would say that she was running away, and maybe she was. But if she was running away, then it was the only way, so she kept moving.

When she was eighteen, someone asked her if she wanted to dance in a strip club, and it didn't take her long to say yes. The money was good, and by this time the walls of her heart were cement and vines, so no problem. It seemed like an easy enough way to get paid, and sex with strangers was no issue. (When you get raped as a child, you usually become a "rape magnet," she said—like it happens again and maybe again at other points. So it's better to control it as best you can with an exchange of money or some nice trip.)

She took off her clothes onstage without much thought or feeling. She smoked weed and drank shots of Jack in order to prepare, but once there, she performed. Sometimes she balked at it all; she thought that she needed to be punished for having had an abortion, and maybe punished for just being herself.

Other times she loved the attention; she found power more intoxicating than alcohol or drugs, and, when used effectively, it had amazingly fruitful results. She could juggle multiple men who chased her, and she could pick and choose as she liked. If it was a man's world, then she would make the most of it.

Within a year, she was pregnant again, and this time she resolved to have the baby. She struggled as a young, single mother but still got into college. She was trying to change for her child; she became a Christian and focused on reconciling the sins of her past. One night, she brought a fellow student home from a bar. He didn't have a way home and asked if he could stay at her place for the night and sleep on her couch. He respected that she needed it to be that way. She had to get her baby from a friend and get her home to bed, but she agreed to help him. This guy seemed okay and settled in on her couch. He thanked her profusely for her kindness and asked her to wake him in the morning. But within an hour, he came into her room and raped her in her bed with the baby just feet away in her crib.

She didn't want to wake the baby! But when she protested, he told her to shut up. When she said, "Please stop," he continued. So she just left her body. She watched herself from above and felt a distant sorrow, but nothing she could clearly understand. *What do I feel?* she asked herself. *Will I be killed? Unclear. Just don't wake the baby. Oh God, how can this be happening right next to my baby? What have I done? Are we in danger? Will he kill us? How do I get rid of him?* She couldn't speak. By this time in her life, she didn't cry anymore. Crying was just too much work, and it never changed a thing.

He fell asleep in her bed. She didn't sleep at all that night.

She lay awake like a sentry on duty—still, she gave him a ride to school in the morning. It was her fault again. She kept making these bad decisions.

Unfortunately, this type of thing was not a completely uncommon event. Some men came disguised as protectors, boyfriends, and lovers, only to use, take, and disappear. If they defined worth, then it slipped through her fingers like sand. There were no words to describe the pain of no meaning. No words to convey the despair of a girl's soul when she was just hanging on and trying to make her life different. But how do you do that when you do not have a guide, a road map, or any clue how to change? How do you do that when no one loves you or believes in you?

She went back to stripping when she was thirty-five. Her boyfriend thought it would be a good idea because her job as a secretary ended when her office closed. He needed her to contribute to their finances, even though he had a good job. She had two kids to feed now, and he didn't want to be responsible for them. She wanted him to be happy, and so she agreed.

The place was packed by 10:00 p.m. when she returned for her first night. The music was loud, Nine Inch Nails wailing. A blond girl was onstage on her hands and knees, tossing her head and hair and swinging her hips to the beat. The string between her legs hid nothing, and from a few feet away it looked as if she were completely naked. One man had his hand on her thigh, caressing, trying to grab a little higher; a small crowd had gathered around her.

Oh God, she thought. *How in the hell am I going to do this?*

She went into the dressing room. Three fucked-up girls

waiting their turn lounged around the mirrored table. She began to change into her quickly put-together costume from another time. Ugh, too much. Oh well, it was coming off soon
enough anyway. Her hands were shaking as she finished getting
ready. The other women were nice enough but didn't pay much
attention to her and continued their conversation. She felt like
an impostor, like someone trying on something that just didn't
fit. Her discomfort was palpable; she looked like a stranger to
herself in the mirror.

"Abby! Your turn!" a voice yelled through the curtain. She
turned and went through the veil that separated the reality from
the illusion. One step, then the other, a few familiar faces in the
crowd—too late to turn back now—she moved into the music
and out of herself. Another woman inhabited her body as she
played the role like she remembered. It began to feel easy, and
she tasted power on her lips as she moved out into the murky
place where what she knew of herself disappeared. There was
nothing else to think about except the dollar bills coming at her
and the rush of being desired. Why had she thought this would
be hard? It wasn't. The money came.

Around 4:00 a.m., the police raided the bar. Evidently,
something out of compliance was going on, and they confis-
cated all of the money from the girls. Everyone was pissed, but
there was nothing to do about it. Someone said it happened
periodically. Who knew if it was legal? They were the police,
after all.

She grabbed her gear and went home. She was tired and had
no money to show for a night's work. All of a sudden, she felt
as if she had been sucked into a nightmare and completely laid

herself out for no gain, only a cost that wasn't entirely clear. She had to take her kids to school in just three hours. Who had she become in this short amount of time? What would she say to Jake when he asked her about the money?

She climbed into bed with him, and he sleepily asked her how it had gone. She told him about the police.

"You're going back, though, baby, right?"

"I don't know," she said. "Probably."

"Good girl," he replied. "Now go to sleep."

She didn't sleep, though. Her hair smelled like cigarettes, and her skin was crawling. She got up and took a shower. Her throat hurt and her body ached. By 10:00 a.m., she had no voice. She had developed the worst laryngitis of her life and could not even whisper. It was uncanny, strange. As the days passed, she became sicker, feverish, still no voice. She couldn't go back to work. Jake called in sick for her. He was frustrated, though. What the hell? How could this be? How could any of this be?

Her voice stayed gone for two weeks. This had never happened before. It became clear to her, in some distant, symbolic way, that perhaps she had gone too far backward, allowed herself to negate her value, given away her voice. . . . Yes. She had not lost her voice, and it had not been taken; this time, she had given it away and fallen back into an old habit that wasn't in her best interest. *Why do we have to repeat and rebuild?* she wondered. But her choice was clear: die or get reborn.

She did not go back to the strip club again. She began to pack. She collected coffee, canned goods, paper products in a box in her closet. She kept her plans secret from Jake. She was skimming off the top of his groceries. Two months later, she packed up her truck and left town with her kids. Jake remained in and out of her life for the next few years, but at least she was choosing to rebuild and live. She found a good job and an apartment and was able to provide for her children. One day, her heart no longer wanted Jake, and she was free of him. It would still always be a temptation, a well-worn groove in the road of life, to want to give it all up for a man, but she knew this now and could work to overcome the habit. She was grateful that her voice had returned, and with that voice, she would make new choices. Life was sometimes painful and lonely, but somehow the choice to live differently embodied a power from deep within that was stronger than the fleeting power the outside world had assigned her. Maybe she could teach her kids differently.

Attachment theory was first developed by the British psychiatrist John Bowlby in the late 1960s, through his work with young children, who, Bowlby noted, learn through their experiences with their adult caretakers and early relationships whether they are lovable or inadequate, and whether or not they deserve to be treated well by others. Bowlby believed that what a child learns about herself from her parents or primary caretakers is likely to affect that child throughout her lifetime, or from "the cradle to the grave."[13]

Many others have built upon Bowlby's work over the years, and we now have a much more complete understanding of how attaching and experiencing love at an early age affect

13. Valerie E. Whiffen, A Secret Sadness (Oakland, CA: New Harbinger Publications, 2009), 59.

a person throughout her life, and how the lack of attachment at an early age manifests itself in numerous, challenging ways throughout the life cycle as well. Attachment theory is also connected to many newer theories about how trauma manifests in a person's life. We will further discuss the impact of lack of attachment and its relationship with sexual exploitation in later chapters, but for the purpose of this chapter, we must note that the loss of voice clearly coincides with a lack of attachment during childhood for many survivors.

Insecurely attached girls believe that their worth as people depends upon their ability to meet the standards and gain the approval of others. Oftentimes, as children, these young women or adult women believe that unless they are "perfect," they will not be loved. They set up unrealistic expectations for themselves that create a web of shame, anxiety, and depression.[14]

The effects of shame cannot be overstated in regard to loss of the voice. The "dirty little secrets" that remain unexpressed in childhood and adolescence bind the silence a little tighter. In her book *A Secret Sadness: The Hidden Relationship Patterns That Make Women Depressed*, psychologist Valerie Whiffen states that shame is an emotion associated with being a victim. Children who have been bullied, controlled, dominated, or abused by another person are likely to develop the residual effects of shame. She also notes that women who were abused as children will most likely feel more shame than other women.[15] When a woman is trapped in her own shame, she expects other people to reject her. Adult women may feel rejected in response to real and imagined maltreatment, and that in turn may make

---

14. Ibid., 71.
15. Ibid., 109–10.

it difficult for them to establish trusting and enduring relationships. In this never-ending cycle of striving and this constant
war with the inner self, some women conclude that it may be
better to remain silent.

CHAPTER 3

PERFECT STORMS

Perfect storm (noun)

   1. A particularly violent storm arising from a rare combination of adverse meteorological factors

   2. A particularly bad or critical state of affairs, arising from a number of negative and unpredictable factors

Yemaya is the goddess of the sea. She is both form and formless. She is the ocean, and yet at times her humanness makes her as gentle as a mountain stream. She is the essence of motherhood. Legend says she appears to those lost at sea, but for now she dwells in the far beyond, watching as the sirens watch.

   Her waves lap against the bows of ships. She rocks her daughters in her strong, soft arms and carries her sons in her bosom. Her depth is incomprehensible. Her voluminous body, full of curves, sways as she moves back and forth, back and forth. Her dark eyes move fervently across the deep; her ears sense the faintest ripple. This night is different. She tries to block out the noise, but she can't. She sees her children being dragged across the sand, shackled and bound, their skin the color of her depths, their tears as wet as the depths of her womb. She recoils in horror as they are beaten and dragged aboard the ships. She weeps as the rise of capitalism is built on the backs of her children. The slave owners thank her for unlimited access to the naked bodies of African women. They laugh among themselves as they pick the women whose bodies they will defile.

One young girl catches Yemaya's eye. She wails as the men prod and poke her body, ripping from her the covering of her native cloth. Yemaya sees the girl's slim hips and soft nipples; she is not a woman yet. She twists and turns in the men's arms, screaming as their laughter grows louder, more intense. They lift from the fires the red-hot iron and wave it before her face, taunting her. She squeezes her eyes tightly shut, but Yemaya will never forget the look of fright and horror that flashes across her face. She screeches as the branding iron tears into her flesh just below her not-yet-budding breast. The men bicker among themselves, arguing over which one is to have her first. "Not to worry," they agree. "There are plenty more." Her legs and arms flailing, she is yanked into a sailor's quarters. He doesn't want to put on a show, doesn't want to have an audience as he forces himself upon her.

Yemaya's anger erupts. Her breath becomes shallow and her heart starts racing. She begins to howl, the waves around her surging and swelling violently. The sirens sense her emotion.

They sit up and begin to stir uncomfortably. Yemaya has lost control many times, but today seems different. She has never felt so helpless. She clasps her fists, and, try as she might, she can't stop the hot, angry tears. Her sobbing rocks the slave ships violently back and forth. She hears the cries of her children then. They are afraid of the ocean, afraid of her. They scream aloud—the screams of rape, of torture, but mostly of fear.

The sirens cry as well, and their cries soothe her somewhat. She has heard their shrieks and their songs for centuries. They wail helplessly as some, freed for just a moment, jump to their death to avoid the torment of captivity. Their pain is familiar, and Yemaya stretches in defeat, her limbs long and black, regal, powerful. She bellows to the slave owners, howls to the heavens, yet no one seems to hear her. But when the sirens whisper, she begins to calm. She will see her children to their destination safely, she decides. She trusts justice will eventually prevail. These actions will not go unpunished. The perpetrators will be sentenced.

She gathers the boats transporting her children. Her gown is the bluest indigo, carefully printed with the white markings of her purity. She wraps her children in her shroud and rocks them gently as they travel. "Do not be afraid to visit me in the depths," she murmurs, knowing that only by diving deep to the bottomless ocean within themselves will they begin to find their healing.

~☯~

The well-documented atrocities of the Atlantic slave trade disturb even the most desperate proprietor. Walter Rodney described the slave trade as capitalism parading without even a loincloth to cover its nakedness. African men and women, as they were sold and bartered, were forced to strip naked and were checked by their purchasers to make sure they were in suitable condition. Captain Richard Drake, an African slave trader for fifty years, described how blacks were examined head to foot, their joints and muscles squeezed, their arms and legs twisted, their breast and groins pinched without mercy. They were then branded with the identifying marks of their owners, using hot irons. Captains, officers, and crew could be sexual predators, and the powerless female slaves were their victims. If they did not consent, they were severely beaten. Furthermore, prominent abolitionist Olaudah Equiano comments that he knew of child rapes: "I have known our mates commit these acts most shamefully, to the disgrace not of Christians only, but of men. I have even known them to gratify their brutal passion with females not ten years old; and these abominations some of them practiced to such a scandalous excess."[16]

The treatment of some human beings as objects or lesser beings—because of a vulnerability, or a perception that their circumstances, class, race, gender, or sexual orientation makes them unimportant—creates a perfect storm for exploitation and abuse.

Racism is one factor among many that connects to sexual exploitation, but, like all the contributing factors, it cannot be ignored. Racism has held huge influence in the pimping culture by connecting power with the exploitation of others—and thereby employing the very tools used against people of color to harm and control others who are different because of gender. It is a vicious cycle of oppression, and all forms of op-

16. Olaudah Equiano, *The Life of Olaudah Equiano* (Mineola, New York: Dover Publications, Inc.), 1999.

pression are linked to one another by the abuse and misuse of power. It is our belief that those who are involved in the cycle of sexual exploitation, whether it is the facilitator or the pimp, the buyer or the person being sold—all are part of the same continuum. All have suffered from some form of trauma that has created the capacity and the agency to participate in the cycle. The stories within the mind that cause pain and distress may be very different, and all are valid; however, the stories might not be helpful or true.

At the SAGE Project in San Francisco, an old poster framed on the wall stated DON'T BELIEVE EVERYTHING YOU THINK. This poster was from one of the first anti–human trafficking campaigns in the country and was featured on San Francisco taxicabs in the 1990s. Its message remains important and relevant, though—our thoughts are not always helpful or true. If we seek to change our habitual thinking and ways of operating in the world, it takes fortitude, an emergence of consciousness, and the willingness to look inward. We can challenge oppression only when we are willing to look at how we unconsciously and consciously participate in the oppressing and judging of others based on how they look, where they came from, or how we perceive them as different.

Human trafficking has been described as a form of "modern-day slavery." This description reflects the very intersections and connections people have made around the abuse of power and the conditions that many who have been trafficked for labor and sex have experienced. Unfortunately, however, this loaded term is often used for emotional appeal and thereby loses its ability to express the complexities and effects of human trafficking, as well as slavery throughout history. Under U.S. law, human trafficking—when applied to adults—is defined by the use of force, fraud, and coercion for both labor and sex.[17] For those under the age of eighteen, any form of commercial sexual exploitation is considered human trafficking. Although most youth will not agree that they are "victims of trafficking,"[18] most *will* agree that events and situations in their lives have made them vulnerable to sexual exploitation. Usually, a perfect storm of events that includes some form of early sexual trauma or traumas is part of the equation that predisposes a person to commercial or noncommercial sexual exploitation.

We must examine sexual exploitation, commercial sexual exploitation, and all aspects of human trafficking within the context of the many other social justice issues that impact them, including racial inequality, educational opportunity, access to health care, and gender discrimination, as well as issues of environmental justice. Women who have been labor-trafficked into the United States are usually sexually abused, raped, or exploited in other ways as well. Not only are they expected to work for free, but they are also expected to service their captors sexually, or they are raped. As long as our society accepts treating people as objects that can be bought and sold, the trafficking of people for both labor and sex will persist.

Rape and sexual battery have been studied and researched by many who have gone before us, paving the way for our examination of sexual exploitation and the trafficking of minors. Rape was the feminist movement's initial paradigm for violence against women in the sphere of personal life. As understanding

---

17. Trafficking Victims Protection Act Reauthorization of 2013, https://www.congress.gov/bill/113th-congress/house-bill/898.
18. Ellyn Bell, "Children Are Always Victims in Sex Trade, but They Won't Always Agree," *Chronicle of Social Change* (September 2013), https://chronicleofsocialchange.org/opinion/children-are-always-victims-in-sex-trade-but-they-wont-always-agree/.

deepened, the investigation of sexual exploitation progressed to encompass relationships of increasing complexity, in which violence and sexual intimacy commingled. The initial focus on street rape, committed by strangers, led step by step to the exploration of acquaintance rape, date rape, and marital rape. The focus on the rape of adults also led inevitably to an acknowledgment of the sexual abuse of children. As in the case of rape, the initial work on domestic violence and the sexual abuse of children grew out of the feminist movement. Services for victims were organized outside of the traditional mental health system, often with the assistance of professional women inspired by the movement.[19] The emergent understanding of the interconnections of rape, child sexual abuse, and domestic violence put the focus right back on the abuse of power, where it belonged. The research that exploded from the movement to address violence against women impacted policy, social welfare, law, and mental health treatment in profound ways. Thankfully, child welfare and childhood sexual abuse are not the taboo topics they once were, either. In a few decades, a movement of courageous women and male allies made enormous strides toward addressing the intersections of violence and oppression.

Unfortunately, despite all this progress toward a deeper understanding of root causes, the world we live in still accepts rape, ironically, perhaps even more so than in the past. Amid a resurgence of rapes on college campuses and a new generation of victim blaming, victim shaming, and discussions about what determines "consent," new movements addressing sexual violence are being born. Some of the rhetoric around the issues is slightly different, and the Internet plays a distinct role, given

---

19. Judith Herman, *Trauma and Recovery: The Aftermath of Violence—from Domestic Abuse to Political Terror* (New York: Basic Books, 1992), 31–32.

people's ability to shame victims in public and online with photos gone viral and social media posts.

"Rape culture," as defined by the Women's Center of Marshall University in Huntington, West Virginia, is "an environment in which rape is prevalent and where sexual violence against women is normalized and excused in the media and popular culture. Rape culture is perpetrated through misogynistic language, objectification of women's bodies, and the glamorization of sexual violence, thereby creating a society that disregards women's rights and safety."[20] This definition pretty much sums up the issues young women face in a culture eager to exploit them and where sexual appeal superficially defines their worth. The lines of consent have been further blurred by the influence and mainstreaming of BDSM,[21] Internet photos "catching" women in compromising situations with men who later assaulted them, and the manner in which the dominant, patriarchal culture teaches and experiences human sexuality. Often, pushed by an unconscious desire to conform or a conscious desire to rebel, young people embrace this misogynistic stigma and become what they are "supposed" to be. The following story illustrates just how such a surrender to this stigma occurs.

"I wanna be a stripper," Little Bit said defiantly. "They make hella money."

The girls laughed. Some covered their mouths, ashamed to be laughing at such absurdity; others snickered loudly in agreement. Little Bit was twelve. Her skin was clear and her eyes still

---

20. Marshall University Women's Center, "Rape Culture," http://www.marshall.edu/wcenter/sexual-assault/rape-culture/.
21. "BDSM" is an acronym for "bondage and discipline, sadomasochism."

bright. Her light-colored hair was pulled back into a high ponytail. She hadn't weathered the same storms of life that many
of the girls had. Yet.

She looked around the circle at all of them. "Whaaat?" she
asked innocently.

"You're stupid as fuck!" declared Reyes. "You think this
is some kinda joke?" She stood up. We sat up straight in our
chairs, poised. Staff moved closer to the doorway. We were
often reminded we were in a locked detention facility. "I wish I
could beat your ass right now and knock some sense into you."
Reyes sat down, as if she, too, remembered in an instant where
she was.

"Don't be mean, Reyes—she's just a kid," one of her peers
said warily.

"I know she's a kid. That's why I want to beat her ass. I
don't think you realize what this life is fuckin' like. It's not like
a damn music video. You don't make hella money, and you
gotta dance in a sweaty, stank-ass club for nasty-ass old men."

"You think I can't do it? You think I can't dance?" Little
Bit asked insolently.

"You're missing the fuckin' point," Reyes said quietly, almost in defeat. It was almost as though she had suddenly remembered herself, remembered where she had been at twelve,
at a time when she herself thought stripping was cool. She
was much older now. She felt much older, at least. Headed to
county jail soon, then likely to the penitentiary, she decided in
this instant that she wasn't going to risk her own vulnerability
in order to save this little kid. Little Bit wasn't her family; she
wasn't her sister.

Reyes put her head in her hands. She thought of her little sister, Nina. The letters and cards she still got from home. The pictures she received—pictures printed out at the library and emailed from Nina's cell phone. Pictures in the bathroom at school: Nina's face made up, shirt a little too low for a twelve-year-old, in Reyes's opinion. Shit, she was growing up.

Little Bit laughed. "I can dance better than most of them hos on the videos." Too afraid to get up, she wiggled her hips in her chair. More giggling.

"They don't care if you can fuckin' dance," said Reyes knowingly. "This ain't *High School Musical*! They care you can take your clothes off and look like a virgin. They hope you ain't, but they want you to look like one!"

This dynamic was becoming normal for us. Young girls new to the facility were trying to fit in. Many times, they were excited by the thought of being "paid" for what had become normalized exploitation in their lives. Older girls, tired of the game, tried to teach them what they knew: that this life was hard, that it wasn't glamorous, that they soon would be tired and used up, that you rarely got paid anyway.

It's too late for me, Reyes wanted to say but didn't. "Just get up out of here and go to damn school" is what came out of her mouth.

Little Bit laughed. "Fuck school." She raised her arms and shook her shoulders. "I'ma dance!"

Reyes rolled her eyes and laughed as well, as did the rest of the group. "I give up," she mouthed.

Although she felt defeated, the words Reyes spoke were more powerful than any we could have shared. What mattered was that, for an instant, Reyes, old enough to be a big sister, wanted to share her wisdom and prevent Little Bit from entering the dark, dismal world Reyes was so familiar with. Little Bit was so young and yet still knew it all. She was herself beyond her years; she had been through so much already, she was no longer afraid. Being in youth detention at her age was a feather in her cap, a stripe on her arm. She wanted to hear war stories from the older girls and learn how to get ahead! She wasn't trying to have some washed-up chick tell her she couldn't dance, couldn't make money.

It was a vicious cycle. We didn't have the answers, but we knew we had to keep plugging away. We had to define for others this perfect storm, this catastrophic collision of circumstances, and then set a new course quickly, or devastation would occur. There would be more shipwrecks and more drowning as a consequence.

Many assert that pornography is about sexual freedom and choice, and those who question the effects of pornography are often characterized as conservative, religious fanatics, or simply anti-sex. Radical feminists of the latter part of the twentieth century tried to frame the argument differently when they moved the conversation away from sexual liberation and toward the eroticization of domination and subordination.[22] Dr. Robert Jensen has done extensive research into pornography and concludes that it is a genre in which the worst aspects of

22. Robert Jensen, "Blow Bangs and Cluster Bombs: the Cruelty of Men and Americans," in *Not for Sale: Feminists Resisting Pornography and Prostitution* (North Melbourne, Australia: Spinifex Press, 2004).

patriarchy, white supremacy, and corporate capitalism come together to form a perfect storm of inequality.

The conversation of pornography is complicated further when it is broadened to include child victims. The sexual abuse of children has now emerged into the light of day as a topic recurring in movies of the week, political debate, television talk shows, and celebrity confessions. At the center of this discovery lies child pornography, which the US Supreme Court considers a gruesomely potent subset of child sexual abuse. Child pornography "whets the sexual appetites of pedophiles, creating their fantasies and stimulating them to victimize real children."[23] Unfortunately, child pornography also plays a part in the sexual exploitation of children and the reasons men are willing to pay top dollar to have sex with a child. Underground markets and hidden areas of the Internet also make for a ripe playing field for this type of exploitation to occur. Around the world, including in the United States, victims are becoming younger and the nature of the exploitation more violent.

We can't talk about human trafficking, prostitution, and the sexual exploitation of women and children without discussing the impact and effects of pornography and a pornographic culture upon our views of sexuality. Gloria Steinem once wrote that "the repression of non-procreative sex in a conservative, male-dominated world perpetuates images—wife or whore, good woman, bad woman," placing special emphasis on the fact that these images assert that the "bad woman," the pornographic model or prostitute, is unprotected by culture and deserving of any violence toward her.[24]

23. Amy Adler, "The Perverse Law of Child Pornography," Columbia Law Review 101, no. 2 (2001): 209–73.
24. Gloria Steinem, "Erotica and Pornography: A Clear and Present Difference," in *Take Back the Night: Women on Pornography*, Laura Lederer, ed. (New York: Morrow and Co., 1980).

But there are huge distinctions between pornography and erotica. The mutually empowering sense of being sexual and enjoying the beauty of the human form is not the problem. The issue is the degradation of another human being for pleasure. Our culture of power-over has created an appetite for this type of sexual gratification, and we have to look at its impact upon how we are sexually stimulated. Unwanted sexual violence toward another person is never acceptable.

The next story illustrates how this commingling of pornographic fantasy and real life—if it does not come from a place of mutuality and respect—can confuse and harm young people as they find their sexual identity.

"What does 'survival sex' mean, anyway?" Summer asked rhetorically. "Sex for a place to stay or for food? Or sex because you are afraid if you don't willingly participate, you might die?"

We were debriefing Summer and a number of other young women on a workshop in which they had participated.

"I mean, at that moment, when you make the decision to fuck him, or fuck them, it's usually because you know, deep down in your heart, you know that they will rape you, or probably kill you, if you allow them to have a taste of your fear.

"It's like a shark getting a taste of blood: once they taste or smell the blood in the water, they fuckin' lose it. They all come then, wanting a piece of the flesh. I figure as long as I'm willing to give them what they want, they won't ever really experience the satisfaction of raping me. I think once they do that, rape won't even be enough. Then they'll really want to kill me. Maybe if I just give 'em what they want, I keep a little piece of dignity, a little piece of power."

Summer continued, "I remember one time, I was fuckin' this guy. It was New Year's, and we were smashed. I knew he really liked me years ago, and I wanted to be in love, you know. I wanted someone to really want me or love me on New Year's. I had called him after the club and made him come get me. I was really excited about spending time with someone I thought was into me. So anyway, we're getting busy in a motel room—I guess he had rented the room for New Year's—and his cousin comes back to the room. But my dude, he doesn't stop what he's doing. He continues to screw me. I know I'm drunk, but I also know this ain't cool. I start telling him, 'Stop, babe, we should stop. I don't wanna do this anymore.'

"He starts laughing, and so does his cousin. Now I'm scared, right, 'cause he's straight bangin' me with this other dude in the room. It seems like he's feeling like a real man right now. He turns me over, and I'm getting even more scared now. He's thrusting even harder. I know his cousin is watching. It's pitch dark, but I can sense the shift in the energy. It's like all my high disappeared and I'm completely sober. I start wondering, *How the hell am I gonna survive this? These dudes is crazy. I'm not even like this; I'm on vacation from college. I'm not this chick.* I start having this conversation with myself, but I don't scream. I don't fight. The cousin moves in closer. It feels like he's a fuckin' shark. I think to myself, *If I allow them to know I'm scared, they will get the taste of blood, and then it's over.*

"I mean, I didn't say a damn thing. I just let them carry

on. He moved in slowly at first, the cousin. He just stood there, inches from my face. Then he grabbed my hair. I was on my hands and knees, and this guy was still fuckin' me from behind. He was starting to hurt me, but I didn't say a word. The cousin shoved his thing in my mouth, you know? It was like we were in a fuckin' porno movie. They were talking to each other, talking about me like I wasn't even in the room. They were egging each other on, encouraging each other, like they were in a damn football game. I half expected that cheesy fuckin' sex-tape music to start playing in the background. I chuckle to myself even now, while retelling the story, except nothing is funny.

"This wasn't a movie, and there was no music. This wasn't sexy, and every inch of my body hurt. He was so far down my throat, I thought I was going to vomit. I kept gagging and crying. They were both ripping at my body, until I felt myself go numb. Like I was in the ocean, getting eaten by savage sea creatures, I just closed my eyes and drifted to the sandy bottom. I tried to imagine the water covering my soul, like I was being buried in a watery grave. The waves grew stronger and tossed me to and fro. I could taste the saltiness of the surf and feel the grainy sand against my skin.

"I don't know how long this continued. Eventually I lifted my head out of the water and took a breath. One of them threw me a towel. The cousin left, I guess, and the guy I was with crawled back into bed and held me in his arms. He said, 'Happy New Year's, baby,' and he went to sleep.

"I didn't say a word to anyone. As I lay there in this guy's arms, I wondered if they were just really drunk. Or maybe I was. Maybe I imagined the whole thing. Maybe this cheap, violent-ass porno that was enacted in this sleazy motel was all a dream.

"I didn't leave until the morning. I had bites all over my neck and chest the next day—not teenage love bites but teeth marks and scratches. I took a shower for hours, trying to scrub the marks away, not the physical marks but the psychological ones. I hoped the hot water would cleanse me. Maybe I could scald away the memories. For many years, I would have anxiety attacks as I drove down the freeway past that old motel. I would see them again from time to time when I would come home from college. No one ever spoke of it. It was never mentioned. I wondered if they thought I was a whore. Was this survival sex? Did I really survive, or did I drown in the deep of the ocean that night?"

As R. Barri Flowers indicates in *Prostitution in the Digital Age: Selling Sex from the Suite to the Street*, "many homeless [or at-risk] girls find themselves engaging in survival sex, defined as the 'commercial sexual activity of young people as a way of obtaining the necessities of life, including food, drugs, clothing, transport, or money to obtain these goods and services.'" Studies indicate up to 50 percent of homeless youth get involved in survival sex, which can often be a prelude to more formal types of prostitution. A perfect storm is created when a vulnerable young person enters a violently sexualized world without adequate parental or adult protection. As Flowers illustrates, "within 36 to 48 hours of a girl becoming homeless, she will be solicited for sex, or persuaded, coerced, recruited or abducted into prostitution or pornography by pimps, customers, gangs, pedophiles or pornographers." Survival sex, in varying forms, is a reality for many homeless and runaway youth.

Remaining homeless for thirty days has been found to be perhaps the single greatest determinant in a street youth's turning to prostitution. More than two million teenagers become homeless every year, creating an abundance of at-risk youth available to perpetrators.[25] The definition of survival sex, however, must be broad enough to include other situations where young people and adult women engage in or are forced into sexual activity in order to survive. By using this broad definition, we do not separate survival sex from other forms of sexual violence. As the societal factors that contribute to sex trafficking become more pronounced, the level of risk to our young people, especially those who have been previously abused or exploited, will increase exponentially. This reality is inescapable unless we begin to address the root of the problem, which at the core is a deep societal sickness around how we treat each other as human beings, including people's problematic relationships with, and lack of insight around, sexuality in general. These societal ills have been influenced by our religious systems, our family structures, our cultures, and a societal love affair with obtaining and holding power, regardless of the cost.

25. R. Barri Flowers, *Prostitution in the Digital Age: Selling Sex from the Suite to the Street* (Santa Barbara, CA: Praegar, 2011), 92.

CHAPTER 4

THE DROWNING

I was much further out than you thought
And not waving but drowning . . .

I was much too far out all my life
And not waving but drowning.

—Excerpt from "Not Waving but Drowning,"
by Stevie Smith[26]

Could it be that Stevie Smith is prophetically describing twenty-first-century America? The global society in which we live; the society we watch projected on our TV or computer screens, curled up comfortably on our couches or covered cozily in our beds. The America that we, as social service providers, watch—as it deteriorates, as kids become vulnerable to exploitations at younger and younger ages, as teens become incarcerated and sexuality becomes more perverse. As teenage girls insist they

---

26. Stevie Smith, "Not Waving but Drowning," in *Collected Poems of Stevie Smith* (New York: New Directions Publishing, 1972).

"choose" to be in the sex industry and the community turns its back, insisting unless a girl is dragged out of a suburban shopping mall and tied to a bed, she must "want" to be a prostitute. More and more, we have become a society in which we have value only if someone wants to purchase us. For many young women, this idea takes on great importance, as value is not established elsewhere or the impact from our highly sexualized culture is too strong to resist. No wonder people are confused.

The young women with whom we work all too often end up far out in the ocean, waving insistently and shouting, *I'm okay!* Frequently, we dive into the water anyway, like athletic young lifeguards in red bathing suits. We swim far out in the deep, risking all we can to drag our young people to shore. Only after many long hours of building relationships, listening, responding, showing up, do they finally feel comfortable enough to mutter, "I was much too far out all my life, and not waving, but drowning." It seems for many girls, this admission will somehow prevent them from ever being able to journey into the ocean again. They worry about the implications of a life on land, when all they have known is the smell of salt water and the brisk ocean air.

America as a society also seems to be drowning, too proud or fearful to admit the trouble we have created. Gender oppression and racism permeate our society, setting the stage for the exploitation of all women, but especially for women of color and of lower socioeconomic status. These women, of all ages, lack the privilege of those who may have more choices when it comes to the industry of sex. Their worth has been implicitly questioned for too many years, by too many people, and their attachments to caregivers or family are tenuous. Because of these sad and altogether-too-common facts, they compromise themselves for the facsimile of love and true care. It can happen to anyone with shaky beginnings, and it makes finding one's way much more difficult.

The community and societal factors that have moved us from the perfect storm into the drowning are plenteous. Issues such as poverty and unemployment breed desperation, not only among women but also the men who choose to exploit them. The International Labour Organization (ILO) said in May 2014 that there were twenty-one million people in forced labor in the world, two-thirds of whom come from the sex industry.[27] Of the profits derived from forced labor per year, $99 billion is generated by the sex industry.[28] Human trafficking has overtaken the illegal-arms industry and risen to become the second-most-profitable criminal enterprise (behind drug trafficking).[29] If the current trends continue, sex-trafficking sales will likely tie or exceed drug sales in the near future—especially since prostitution and drugs, for many, go hand in hand.

The lack of institutional support, especially in the United States, among courts, law enforcement, and social service organizations for survivors of the sex industry remains problematic. There are simply not enough services for this demographic, and oftentimes the services aren't relevant to the needs of those

27. International Labour Organization, "Forced labour making 150 bn dollar proht—ILO Report," May 19, 2014, http://www.ilo.org/global/about-the-ilo/newsroom/news/WCMS_243201/lang--en/index.htm.
28. Ibid.
29. State of California Department of Justice, Office of the Attorney General, "Human Trafficking," http://oag.ca.gov/human-trafficking.

whose lives have been impacted by prostitution and the sex industry in general. All too often, a dichotomy exists between those who identify as advocates for sex workers and those who identify as advocates for "survivors." This dichotomy ignores that both groups, regardless of how they identify or whether they choose or don't choose to remain in the industry, need appropriate services in order to help them to take care of themselves, avoid violence, and have access to other choices in life.

Our childhood traumas set the stage for much of the pain that we experience in adulthood and, if unresolved, pull us under in currents we can neither see nor understand. At some point, many a bright and promising woman finds herself pulled under the water, unable to surface for air. The metaphor of drowning captures the eerie numbness of going under and being unable to breathe or find one's way out. The following story is about an actual near drowning that rings true as a metaphor for traumas that occur when we are children and imprint their residual effects on our psyches. We carry these long-buried memories into our adult lives and live them unconsciously until a time when we are able to see them and their imprint more clearly.

The rope around her neck and torso did not give; the moving boat was too fast, and the water rushing around her too strong. She was only ten but a skilled swimmer, water skier, and tomboy girl unafraid of adventure. But today the adventure had turned dangerous. She had fallen while ski sledding double with a friend, and the towrope had wrapped itself around her neck and back. The force of the still-moving boat dragged her little body through the water. Her face just inches below the surface, she could still see sunlight but could not come up for air. After only a decade of life, she felt as if it were ending as her struggling body began to relax into a strange numbness, and then the boat stopped. Her head surfaced, and she felt the air on her face again—a gasp of breath. They grabbed her arm and pulled her into the boat, but no one spoke of her near drowning, no one acknowledged her fear, and so she internalized the message that her life had little meaning to those around her who were supposed to care.

Many years later, she remembered the feeling of being underwater, without the ability to surface, and at the same time able to see sky and sunlight. The man whom she loved the most, the one with whom she had dropped all her boundaries—intoxicated by the sweetness of his professed "love"—was the same man who lied to her, cheated on her, verbally abused her, endangered her numerous times, and without words threatened to disappear if she continued to question his misdeeds. This man drove the new boat, dragging the new rope that securely held her body just enough under the water that she could not surface for breath; she knew then that her life had little meaning to he who was supposed to care.

Long ago, through experiences of insignificance mixed with periods of care and attention, she had learned to take the latter as medicine to keep her feeling alive and worthy. When a man offered her money for sexual services, she thought she was receiving attention and worth. Cash spoke volumes under the water. When a lover held her in his arms and called her "the special one," she felt for a moment the safety that she lacked inside herself and, for a minute, the feeling that she might resurface.

Pimps, like abusive lovers and sex-addicted narcissists, often ensnare their victims by creating a false atmosphere of love, attention, and intense desire. This is the reason so many young women who come from families where appropriate safety and security are not present are highly vulnerable to the conditioning and pretense of a boyfriend-pimp. When he begins to ask her to engage in more and more dangerous or risky behaviors, it is usually after a period of grooming her to believe that she is special, unique, and his most desired one. It might begin with sex in public or a blow job in the parking lot of a grocery store during broad daylight. He convinces her that this is normal and is the way she can show him that she loves him. He lets her know that this is what the "chosen one" does, and the unspoken threat is that if she does not comply, then she will be replaced. Eventually, he convinces her that having sex with other men and giving him the money she earns is also a sign of a deep and enduring love bond. But the bond is only one-way, and she is silently drowning.

In some ways, sex work itself feels like power. It is the power of worth in action for services rendered. Sexual promiscuity holds some of this same power, but it is not quite the same as the power of cash, which speaks of worth like nothing else in this world. If you do not feel valued for the person that you are, then you might as well be paid.

When a person has been subject to a combination of subtle and intermittent abuses, combined with perceived love and declarations of love, attention, and care, a most confusing message is sent. This combination occurs in emotionally abusive relationships, love triangles, and sexually exploitive relationships. It occurs in the lives of women who have been sex workers, women who have been molested as children, and women who have been raped or assaulted by people they loved and trusted, and in all relationships where power over another is used and manipulated. It is not love but a lie, a trauma bond and a rope around the neck that pulls a girl under. This is drowning.

We have lingered in the chambers of the sea
By sea girls wreathed with seaweed red and brown
Till human voices wake us, and we drown.[30]

— T. S. Eliot

"Right here, right here where it says 'ethnicity'"—the girl pointed to the sign-in sheet for one of our girls' groups weekly With Respect and Passion (WRAP) sessions—"I put 'MB.'"

"'Mexican and black?'" Stacey asked.

"No!" She laughed. "'Mixed breed.'"

"'Mixed breed? ' Stacey asked again, sent immediately back to the labels of her childhood: mixed breed, mixed race, mulatto.

"Yeah, I'm a mixed breed." The girl laughed again.

We talked about it later. Stacey, frustrated, thought, as she

30. T. S. Eliot, "The Love Song of J. Alfred Prufrock," in *The Wasteland and Other Poems* (New York: Harcourt Brace Jovanovich, 1934), 3.

always had when she was a child, *What is a mixed breed? What am I, some kind of dog? Some kind of animal?*

In our minds, we looked around the room at the diversity of the girls. We were used to seeing black and Mexican girls in group; we hadn't really considered the number of "mixed" girls among us. Stacey shared her own story of identity issues and struggles with fitting in. We thought also of our good friend, a survivor, who in her testimony called out the fact that she is "mixed" as a precipitating risk factor in her story of exploitation. Could this be true? Could the issue of race go beyond color lines of black and brown women, the underclass, those of us who are not worthy of anything more than being sex toys or sexual slaves? Could the issue of identity also play a part in the likelihood of a girl's susceptibility to the manipulation of a pimp or a perpetrator, or even her being chosen in the first place?

Renowned developmental psychologist Erik Erikson, in his eight-stage model of psychosocial development, defines how adolescents typically behave in the fifth stage, Identity vs. Role Confusion.[31] During the teen years, young people endeavor to discover the essence of who they are as a person, what they stand for, and where they want to be in their future.[32] Childhood wounds and even trauma during this important stage of transition affect not only how youth feel about themselves but how they imagine the rest of the world to feel about them as well.

Young people of color progress through the same identity stages Erikson describes; however, they also progress through the development of their individual cultural identity, which, again, is at the very core of their being. This progression within

---

31. Erik Erikson, *Identity and the Life Cycle* (New York, NY: W. W. Norton & Company.
32. Glenn Jordan and Chris Weedon, *Cultural Politics: Class, Gender, Race, and the Postmodern World* (Hoboken, NJ: Wiley-Blackwell, 1995), 275.

a dominant society that does not support or understand their cultural distinctiveness, as well as within a family that doesn't support or understand them, can be extremely difficult.

Negrophobia, a pathological fear of black people, seems also to be a recurrent theme in the current US human-trafficking movement. The "moral panic" fueled by the hysterical phobia of the black male pimp in the United States appears to have reached epidemic proportions. Marketing the trafficking movement by instigating white fear of the Negro pimp has resulted in this phenomenon's lucrativeness for many social service organizations and ministries. This appears to be especially true in more rural or predominately Christian fundamentalist areas of the country.

Like sexual violence, racism is fundamentally related to power and domination, control and exploitation. Racist discourse and imagery are actually an afterthought. Pimps or facilitators, of any age, race, and ethnicity, assume psychological, biological, social, and economic control over the lives of the women they sell. Similarly, women who have been involved in varying conditions of domestic violence describe issues of control and power, captivity and deprivation. Teens describe horrendous abuses at the hands of their pimps, woven with intermittent periods of perceived intimacy, connection, tenderness, and "love." Most times, pimps and domestic perpetrators use this unpredictability as part of their intense manipulation. Many abused women and victims of child abuse and/or exploitation never find the fortitude to follow through with pressing charges and testifying against the person they love. Pimps and perpetrators of all kinds use brainwashing techniques. These techniques include social isolation, torture, threats, the capricious enforcement of rules, drugging, and forced addiction with occasional reprieves and indulgences. The intermittent nature of the abuse makes it confusing and difficult for a traumatized person to leave. She may want to remember only the "good" times, when the abuser was kind and loving, and make excuses for the bad behavior. Thus, cognitive dissonance results in many who have been abused and exploited.

As feared as the black (or of-color) male pimp is, women of color are also defined by their perceived exoticism. In the eighteenth and nineteenth centuries, Europeans became obsessed with the "sexual appetites" and "primitive genitalia" of African women. Saartjie Baartman, the Hottentot Venus, may have been the most famous black woman of the nineteenth century; her body became an obsession, her large breasts, buttocks, and labia put on display for men and women alike.

It is true that being female and black, or brown, is a double bind that causes even the most healthy and intelligent among us at times to question our identity and self-worth against the backdrop of paternalism. For some ethnicities—Asian women, for example—their "exotic" look is seen as merely "erotic" in a society such as ours, where they have become the sexual fantasy of many men. Sadly, for many sex buyers or players, women are so objectified that their race or ethnicity becomes either a smorgasbord of choices to sample or completely irrelevant, and for pimps, money green is the only color that really matters.

In situations of captivity, the perpetrator becomes the most powerful person in the victim's life, and his actions and beliefs shape her psychology. The perpetrator's first goal seems to be the enslavement of his victim; he accomplishes this by exercising despotic control over every aspect of the victim's life. But simple compliance rarely satisfies him, as he appears to have a psychological need to justify his crimes, and for this he needs the victim's affirmation; thus, he relentlessly demands professions of respect, gratitude, or even love. His ultimate goal appears to be the creation of a willing victim. Hostages, political prisoners, battered women, and slaves have all remarked upon the captor's curious psychological dependence on his victims. Sex offenders demand that their victims find sexual fulfillment in submission. For the pimp, a willing victim means complete loyalty and the continued ability to do business.

Many girls become so brainwashed by their pimps that they begin to believe in the game and bend its rules to their own advantage. These girls describe returning to juvenile halls or temporary shelters to recruit other girls, and thus becoming essentially both the pimp and the perpetrator. Depending on the pimping structure, these girls may continue to answer to an older male or develop a network for themselves, often on the Internet. In essence, this is the way these young people make sense of their own victimization. As the next story, from one of our girls' groups, illustrates, this shift in roles can be very subtle but is an effective means of protection at times.

"It's her fault," Marri yelled defiantly. "She the one who wanna lay on her back."

The girls giggled.

Here we go again, Stacey thought. *Creating safety in group: square one!*

In an open-ended group, it is always hard to form a safe place for young people, especially when they don't really know what safety is. In a youth detention setting, a community of girls who have had to fight for survival, it is even more challenging; they understand the need to learn the rules of the game and to win at all costs. Girls who have often had to learn these rules within their own families now play, or try to play, the game with one another and, of course, with us.

There were few rules—"don't snitch" was the primary mandate—and whatever rules there were kept changing and shifting. Sometimes multiple games were played all at once. We always developed group rules, or agreements, together at the beginning of each session, even if there were no new girls. We talked about respect, confidentiality, and participation. We tried, in the few minutes we had, to develop a common language and shared understanding and to secure a commitment from everyone, though group was always voluntary.

Marri was clearly dancing on the edge. We gave her "the look," as did some of the young people. She wouldn't budge.

"I'm just saying," she said, now even more animated, "If she wanna get paid for fuckin', who are we to step in her way?" She looked around the room. Girls were nodding. "I mean, po-lice, rescue, what is all this bullshit?" The girls now nodded more furiously and began to murmur in agreement—the infamous peer pressure. "Ain't nobody forcing these hos."

"Yeah, I didn't have no damn pimp."

"I ain't gonna lie, Ms. Stacey," said Luna, laughing. "I get a rush when I turn that trick and know I'ma get those kicks or that purse."

We got it instantly. She felt empowered. She was advocating for her own needs. She was being resourceful. But we also got something else. We knew some things she didn't know we knew. We knew her mother. We knew her family. We knew some of her foster parents. We knew her background, as we knew the backgrounds of many of our foster youth. We had been working in the area for a long time. We knew Luna had grown up in the system. We knew the allegations of sexual abuse that had sent her stepfather to prison. We knew her mom was an OG, a local legend, who had sold dope and run streets for most of her life, except when she, too, was incarcerated. She had maybe even sold own daughter at a very young age to various men for drugs. We knew the devastation the whole family had endured. If we had known back then all that we know now about child sexual exploitation, we might have been able to change Luna's trajectory, but, as it stood, her behavior was predictable. She was involuntarily acting out with what seemed like voluntary behavior.

Marri laughed out loud. It was as if she stood up in all of our faces and said, *I told you so!* Her sidekicks clucked and snickered as if they were in a B movie.

We settled the group down and renegotiated respect. Ellyn read a piece about unexpressed pain that weighs you down like an anchor.

One of the new girls spoke up. Ellyn had known her from her work with homeless youth, and their history together may have given this girl comfort and courage.

"I did it, you feel me?" she said. "I mean, sometimes I did it for the money . . . but mostly I did it because that's all I knew." The group was silent. "Sometimes I did it 'cause I was excited about those Js or that purse, and then I ended up not getting shit! I mean, I would feel powerful—like, *I just made hella money*—but at the end of the day, I didn't have shit. I didn't even have my soul."

Luna spoke, uncharacteristically timidly: "Yeah, I never did get that bag. That day, some dude robbed me, then this motherfucker gonna beat my ass and make me go make my money back."

Marri watched in silence.

What ensued was intense dialogue, girls sharing horrific stories of rape, violence, torture, sometimes at the hands of relatives when they were just small children.

After a while, Ellyn began to wrap up the discussion. We always closed the open wounds; talked about self-care, journaling, and referrals; and had a minute of meditation.

Marri started shifting in her seat. "I got something to say," she said loudly.

We stole a glance at each other and at the clock. We weren't going back down this road again.

"I was one of those girls," she said.

We were confused. Adhering closely to the code, she hadn't shared a lot about her prior experiences.

"I mean, I had girls working for me."

We tried hard to stay focused. Our minds were racing. We had lots of girls who had admitted to recruiting, but Marri was so adamantly against prostitution. . . . *Ohhh, we get it!*

"I used to just hustle, you know, some sacks here and there. But then my brother's girlfriend needed someone to have her back out there on the street. I ended up with a few girls. I racked up, but I would get so mad at them. I couldn't understand why they wanted to do that. I mean, who am I to turn down free dough?" The girls weren't shocked. Maybe they already knew. "Really, out there, it's pimp or be pimped." She shook her head. "I ain't finna hit the track, so . . ." Now she was quiet.

We talked with several of the girls after group, including Marri. She seemed so confused. As she was learning the other girls' actual stories, life as she knew it was shifting. She was beginning to feel empathy. It was more than slightly uncomfortable for her, but we knew she had turned a corner.

Inanna heard the call. What woman has not heard it, whether she followed and went down the rabbit hole or not? The call was made, and she, who knew herself as Queen, shed the comfort of her known days and followed.

"From the Great Above she opened her ear to the Great Below. . . . My lady abandoned heaven and earth to descend to the underworld. . . ."[33]

Ancient Sumerians, long before the birth of Christ, knew the tale of Inanna, the Queen of Heaven, who knew no protection of men. She traveled to the underworld to see her sister, Erishkigal, Queen of the Underworld, and her queendom of loneliness, rage, insatiable longing, and despair. No one

33. Diane Wolkstein and Samuel Kramer, *Inanna, Queen of Heaven and Earth* (New York: Harper & Row, 1983), 52.

emerged from this land; no one returned alive. As with many journeys, Inanna had to embark upon it even though she knew not exactly why. And as with many journeys, once she embarked upon this one, there was no turning back, so she was required to follow the unknown path to its unknown conclusion. Stripped along the way of all her power as she knew it, she gave it up, not as acquiescence, but as surrender.

The underworld of a damaged woman's psyche is much like the hell of the underworld Inanna traveled—fraught with demons who threaten to destroy and take from her all that seems to protect her and all that she has so skillfully acquired in the outer world. Inanna was taken to the point of her nothingness and left for dead by Erishkigal, who was a queen in her own right but whose pain was so great that she grieved for no one but herself, had no pity on her sister of privilege and power, and so turned away to let the other woman die alone in pain.

On a meathook in Hell, Inanna hung naked and unmourned, her skin a sallow shell, her eyes without light, her power and her beauty gone. Meanwhile, Erishkigal cried for her own losses, for her inability to feel anything other than despair. Unloved, unattached, uncared for, and forgotten, Erishkigal was the flip side of Inanna, the alter personality. She was compulsive, cruel, and sexually insatiable. Of course she was—how could she be other? She had not been loved properly, and in her ambivalent and confused longing lay the key to her insatiability. In the neo-Assyrian story of Erishkigal and Nergal, they copulated for six days and six nights, yet when Nergal departed, Erishkigal still longed for more—her desire for love was so great, her needs so unaddressed, and her life so bereft of affection.[34]. She was the parallel of today's women, young and old alike, who have experienced this dark and oh-so-lonely place within.

If you have been mistreated, and your soul and body disregarded as unimportant and expendable from an early age, then naturally you long insatiably for love. If some pretense of love is shown to you and is first realized sexually, then you naturally gravitate toward achieving fulfillment of love in this same way. Again and again you may try, but the results never provide the fruit you expect or want. Love cannot be attained by sexually fulfilling the desires of another at your own expense, and yet this truth is too easily forgotten.

Erishkigal can be understood as the neglected other side of Inanna. She is the one who was abandoned by parentage and lost her childhood. She is the consequence of her circumstances, full of rage, greed, and desperation.[35] Inanna is dying and Erishkigal is crying; perhaps both are near destruction. But when spirit creatures called the *kurgarra* and the *galatur* enter the underworld on their stealth journey, they give their compassion and empathy to Erishkigal. They bond to her pain and hear the cries of her wounded heart. Erishkigal is transformed by their understanding and grants them their wish to free Inanna, who is at once released and allowed to go home. It is a spiritual transformation and a rebirth for both queens, when destruction seemed the only way out.

Ninshubar, a spiritual warrior, guides Inanna home with her unflagging loyalty and love. She stands firm, waiting and burning the oil of believing, when all hope is lost. The point

34. Ibid., 158.
35. Ibid.

of Inanna's journey is for her to connect with her own wholeness—all that is broken, all that is lost, must be put together again. As tenuous as this adventure is, both queens could have succumbed to the perils of their pain, but instead they integrate the aspects of the Great Above and the Great Below and find what is whole within. In their near drowning, three aspects of the strong woman are found and brought together: the queen who represents power and beauty, the queen who knows only pain and rejection, and the spiritual warrior who refuses to quit and who carries the lamp, knowing only the fight of hope and the promise of triumph.

The journey to the underworld is the tale of drowning—of losses along the way, of breath and alterations of consciousness, of the silence and heaviness of water, of sad and profound thoughts, and of the last-ditch desire to surface before all is lost completely. And still, the release to the water is sometimes easier than the call back to the surface. The death that occurs when one chooses the known, even if the known no longer serves, is sometimes less frightening than the call to life on the other side.

The story that follows illustrates the near drowning of a young woman and her way back to the surface and the shore.

Her mother watched her go under, but she couldn't save her. She didn't know how. The girl was only fourteen, the same age the mother had been when she began experimenting with drugs, covering hurt with numbness, having sex with grown men, and learning well the whoring way. She didn't want this life for her child. In her single-mother years, her married "find a dad for you" years, and all the years she had worked to redeem herself through education, professionalism, fighting for grand social causes—in all of her overachieving attempts to be of worth—she never imagined her daughter would fall the same way, and it hurt her soul.

The mother had attempted to shield the girl from the whoring life. But it had been for naught, it seemed. The girl was using drugs, and, unlike her mom, she had no shut-off switch. She was an addict from the start. She went to spend time with her biological dad and was molested by an adult man on a camping trip. First strike. She began to use methamphetamine, and she lost herself to the drug. Second strike. The mother left the girl's adopted dad for another man after having an affair with him, and though she had been trying to keep it all together and hide her inadequacies, she suddenly imploded again, sabotaging her entire family and unintentionally hurting her children, as she had always feared she would. Third strike. So it was no big surprise when the little girl went far out to sea and decided not to return.

This is how it began. In time, she followed in the mother's footsteps and became hard and mean inside. She struck out at the mom, stole from the family, hated the mom, cursed the mom. She worked for escort services and massage parlors, made porn videos in back rooms—"red-booked" herself—lying all the time to family, while everyone knew the truth, though they said nothing.

The mom felt shame about the girl and shame about herself. She had failed, as everyone had said she would. One of those self-fulfilling prophecies, she seemed no better than the mother who had given her away when she was a baby. In those days, the mom had figured that she should've given her own daughter a better chance with someone else. She'd figured that she would never be more than less-than.

The war between them went on for years. In fact, after some time, the mom thought she would never like again this child whom she had borne. She didn't want to see her daughter, so, like her own birth mother, she pretended that the girl did not exist. She did not see her. She did not miss her. She forgot about her as best she could, her heart one of stone. She became a pillar of salt. Her carefully constructed past, which she had been trying to forget, haunted her in the actions and life of her daughter. She did not think she could bear it, so she ignored the girl's cries for help, thinking there were none. As in Stevie Smith's poem, she ignored what she thought was waving. But the girl was drowning.

Her daughter found her way back, but it took at least ten years, and the reparation of a sacred mother-daughter relationship, piece by piece—the learning to trust one another again, the communication connection, the attempts to understand—took much attention and a complete willingness to be honest and to stay present to each other through the heartache. This, they learned to do together, and they both grew as humans from it.

The mother is a survivor. The daughter is a survivor, too. Like her mother, she saved herself. She grabbed onto the pieces of driftwood and various lifeboats that offered themselves to her through the fog and mist. She did not drown.

PART II

SHIPWRECKS

CHAPTER 5

THE WOUNDING

It has been said, "time heals all wounds. . . ." The wounds remain. In time, the mind, protecting its sanity, covers them with scar tissue and the pain lessens. But it is never gone.
—Rose Kennedy[36]

No one who is born into this life escapes being psychically wounded in some way. However, the degrees and depths of the wounds suffered, and the time in life when the original wounding occurs, appear to make a significant difference in how that wound affects one's way of living and thinking.

A wound by definition is an injury that causes pain and requires attention and care in order to mend and heal. Psychic wounds are no different than physical wounds, with the exception that a psychic wound cannot necessarily be seen or detected at a glance and doesn't heal as quickly as a physical wound. Unless psychic wounds are properly cared for, they may in fact not heal at all.

36. http://www.goodreads.com/quotes/140515-it-has-been-said-time-heals-all-wounds-i-do

Ideally, people avoid experiencing a serious psychic wounding until they are past childhood, although this seems to be getting more difficult, given how many children today are exposed to situations that catapult them into adulthood long before they are developmentally ready. The earlier the original deep wounding, the more likely it is to imprint the mind and affect the life choices and thinking of the child as she develops. These psychic wounds affect the child's sense of self-worth and identity and her ability to give and receive love—primary factors needed to become a healthy individual and make good life choices. This is why we see so many children deeply injured by trauma on a level that is challenging to address. The psychic wound or trauma that is experienced when a person's core self has been injured at an early age, in an act of extreme disregard, neglect, or sexual or physical violence, has direct repercussions that reverberate throughout a lifetime. These are not easy consequences to address and sometimes go undetected for years. A form of silent suffering is often internalized and is found lying just below the surface of every thought and decision of someone who has endured deep wounding at an early stage of life. The long-term effects of psychological or emotional wounding from childhood and adolescence often last unresolved into adulthood, providing constant context for current situations; they affect how a person interprets any situation, whether positively or negatively.

Childhood wounds are particularly dangerous because, unlike wounds suffered in adulthood, the mind and body remembers them as absolute facts and they thus become part of the story of the victim's life. For instance, adult children of alcoholics learn at an early age how to navigate around other people, anticipating and watching the behavior of caretakers in order to remain safe. This early behavior is a survival mechanism at a young age, but as life progresses, the behavior that once served them well becomes a problem for their self-esteem and personal boundaries in adult relationships.

If the wound of childhood has not healed, then it is often repeated over and over again in various ways and with different actors. How many times do you notice that you make the same unhealthy choices or face the same rejection, hurt, or abuse over and over? The way a person deals with psychological trauma varies and can manifest in numerous coping strategies and defenses, including numbing oneself with substances, sex, or other addictions, as well as dissociating and creating ways to deny the abuse and rewrite the story so it is easier for the mind to comprehend.

So what is the precipitating factor that wounds a child or adolescent and leaves a legacy of reopening the wound throughout a lifetime? Abandonment of any type, as well as sexual, verbal, emotional, or physical abuse, leaves a person with deep wounds. Traumatic events such as accidents, sudden death, and extreme violence have a huge impact on any person, but they can deeply and permanently wound a child who has not cultivated the resources or capacity to process such an event. These traumas may differ in content or cause, but they have a reverberating impact throughout the physical system, imprinting the mind and causing lasting damage to a young psyche.

Judith Herman's groundbreaking book *Trauma and Recovery: The Aftermath of Violence—from Domestic Abuse to*

Political Terror has changed the way we think about and treat traumatic events and trauma victims.[37] Anyone interested in understanding more about sexual exploitation and trafficking, and traumatic responses to these atrocious stressors, must develop an understanding of the depths of trauma in, and an appreciation for the links between, child abuse, rape, and other, more "visible" traumas, such as being prostituted. The tendency for many in this seemingly "new" field of child trafficking is to conduct research and develop programs, absent of a profound understanding of the research and progress that have gone before them. Work like Herman's can provide a strong foundation for additional research into the polyvictimization of child trafficking victims and the types of support that can be beneficial to them.

Trauma, especially the multiple traumas of child abuse and sexual exploitation, attacks one's sense of safety. The fight-or-flight response is on high alert and often intensifies with a "freeze" response, a form of dissociation that acts in opposition to the fight-or-flight tendency to either engage in combat or run away. Many women have described "freezing" even in intimate relationships with seemingly "safe" partners, especially when certain sexual triggers are present. Trauma survivors also often have trouble negotiating boundaries with intimate partners, and subsequently, as we'll describe in future chapters, many find themselves choosing risky situations unconsciously. Sometimes, as a result of their brokenness and the inability to recognize red flags and risk factors, they find themselves in situations that mirror the abuse they experienced as children.

Girls forced to grow up too fast often experience trauma in early intimate relationships that mimic the safety that wasn't

---

37. Herman, *Trauma and Recovery.*

available in their childhood. As a result, situations such as the following story unfold and set the stage for other abuses to occur.

I had a kitten once. She was just a baby, a few months old. I had rescued her and bathed her and made sure she was clean. I was so lonely, I just needed someone. Someone who wouldn't leave me, who would look up to me, who would hold me close and make me feel loved. She was black and gray and had little white socks on her feet. I called her Boots. I had been asking God for a friend. After all, I was miles away from home and so alone. I felt like she was an answer to my prayer. She was my friend—my only friend.

Well, my boyfriend didn't like cats! He said they were nasty and had fleas. She didn't have fleas. He told me to get rid of her, but I wouldn't. I defied him. I don't know if he really hated her or just hated the fact that I loved her and didn't obey him.

One morning he came into my room really early—he had been out all night. Boots and I were curled up in my bed, sleeping. She would curl up on my chest like an infant. I would hear her purring and feel her pawing my skin. We were so content. We needed each other. Well, when he came home and saw her on me, he went off. He screamed at the top of his lungs, and I woke with a start. My heart started pounding, and I began to shake.

He said, "I thought I told you get rid of that damn dirty-ass cat."

I cried and said, "She's not dirty—I bathed her."

He snatched her little body up in one hand and stormed out of the house. "If you won't get rid of her, I will!" he said, and took off down the road.

I ran after him. I was barefoot and in my nightclothes. I was crying, "Stop, baby, I'm sorry, I'll get rid of her; I'll find her a home. Please give her back to me."

He was running down the street, and I was chasing after him. How nobody noticed, I don't understand. It was daylight, and cars were driving by, I'm sure. We lived on a busy street with cars full of people headed to school or work, in their normal way, as part of their normal lives.

After about a block and a half, he stopped abruptly and turned around. His eyes were flaming; rage shot out of his eye sockets like missiles. I was so afraid, I stopped chasing and started to slowly back up.

"You want the fuckin' cat?" he screamed.

"Yes," I whimpered.

"You want this filthy fuckin' animal?"

"Yes, please, baby," I said, my voice a whisper.

Then, as though he were a man possessed, he lifted his hand slowly above his head. I remember it, even now, in slow motion. Her legs were flailing, trying to catch onto his sleeve or his hand.

"You want this damn cat?" he asked again.

I nodded. I couldn't even speak. My voice was frozen in time.

Then, with all his might, he slammed her little body onto the ground. She hit the pavement, and her head exploded. There was blood everywhere. She was dead. He killed her. He killed my cat. He killed my friend. I froze for what seemed like an age; then I turned and ran. I ran and ran and ran. I couldn't stop running and I couldn't stop crying. I was angry and sad and scared all at once. I knew at that moment he had the capacity to kill me, too.

I never told anyone he killed my cat. I didn't walk down that street for weeks. I took the long way around to the store. I felt so helpless and disgusted, even with myself—why hadn't I listened and found her another home; why hadn't I hid her better; why hadn't I gone and cleaned up the sidewalk and given her a proper burial? I had just left her there and saved myself.

He's in prison now for the attempted murder of another woman. I knew he would have killed me, too, if I hadn't obeyed. From then on, I did everything he said. He didn't want me for long, though. He had other girls he pimped out. He didn't even want me for that.

I never forgot the look in his eyes when he killed my cat. It may not seem like much—after all, some say, it was just a cat. But to me, she was my friend. She was the only friend I had. She was maybe even a part of me. Maybe a part of me even died, too. I didn't have another pet, or another friend, for a very long time.

Violence or murder threats against pets are not uncommon in child abuse or other abusive situations. Many survivors describe being forced to witness the sadistic abuse of animals, which leaves them in constant fear for their own lives.[38]

Many of the teens we have worked with have described witnessing horrendous, unpredictable brutality against animals

38 Ibid., 98.

growing up; it has set the stage for many of them to become abusive to animals themselves. Judith Herman reiterates that abused children are often full of rage and sometimes aggressive. These children frequently lack verbal and social skills for resolving conflict, and they approach problems with the expectation of a hostile attack. In our work with detained youth, it was quickly apparent the girls could go from zero to sixty in less than five seconds. Seemingly innocent questions or comments could send them over the edge quickly. A perceived slight from a friend or a missing personal item brought on suspicion and anger. Once they had erupted and experienced the speedy consequence of their "bad" behavior (mace, takedowns, reprimands), they calmed down. They were now comfortable with the fact that they had deserved and received their swift punishment, though at the same time they became only more hostile and angry that they had again been targeted. The cycle continues.[39]

As a child struggles to understand the trauma she has endured, she often turns to self-blame, habitually concluding that her innate badness is the cause of her suffering. If somehow she has brought this fate upon herself, then somehow she has the power to change it.[40] The insistence these girls make that they have *chosen* to "prostitute" themselves is almost inescapable. It is as though they rationalize, *If I choose to be a prostitute, then I can choose to stop.* To admit powerlessness is to take away the very essence of their power.

What young people and adult women often do not understand, however, is the power of the wound. In cases of sexual exploitation, as in cases of domestic violence, perpetrators uti-

---

39. Judith Herman and L. Terr, *Too Scared to Cry* (New York: Harper & Row, 1990), 104; K. A. Dodge, J. E. Bates, and G. S. Pettit, "Mechanisms in the Cycle of Violence," *Science* 250 (1990): 1678–83.
40. Herman, *Trauma and Recovery*, 103.

lize the power of many previous wounds to control their victims and place them in captivity. A single traumatic event, explains Herman, can occur almost anywhere, while prolonged, repeated trauma occurs only in circumstances of captivity. When victims have the freedom to escape, they will not endure additional abuse. In the case of many of the stories of adult women and child survivors, multiple traumas, wounds upon wounds, have occurred, keeping victims captive not in physical bondage but in emotional and psychic slavery. In situations of domestic violence, child abuse and prostitution, barriers to escape are generally invisible.[41] As we discussed in Chapter Three, some of these are systemic barriers (racism, sexism, poverty, gender oppression), but many are psychological. Children, and often women, are rendered captive by their condition of dependency.

Occasionally, we encountered challenging evenings while providing groups for detained girls. On one such night, the girls were talking over one another, each wanting a chance to be heard. Unfortunately, amid all the talking there wasn't any listening going on. We wanted to bring them back to the topic of the evening, which was healthy relationships, but we were finding it hard to keep them on track.

Stories of childhood abuse were the norm that night, strange and fearful memories that leave a mark of shame and hurt and instigate a pattern of covering the wound. Grandpas turning on porn channels and pulling six-year-old girls onto their laps; stepfathers and daddies, mom's boyfriend or an uncle—heavy

41. Ibid., 74.

breathing and hands under jammies and little-girl clothes, fingers inside prepubescent vaginas, and penetration into bodies not fully formed. We've heard versions of these stories repeatedly, but most girls never told anyone until recently. They didn't want to get anyone in trouble with the law, and they didn't want any fallout with Child Protective Services or any other system of so-called "care."

On this night, Erika said, "Do you want to know what happened to me? It was my grandpa, and he did stuff to me, you know, like put his hands all over me. We didn't know what he was doing. He was our grandpa! I never told no one until last year, and then no way the police—it would hurt the family. Anyway, he did it to my sister and cousin, too."

Various girls chimed in.

"My mama is a straight-up ho—she had me in prison, and I didn't live with her until I was six when she got out. She sold me to a man for some cocaine—who does that? That's fucked up! I mean, who sells their kid for drugs? Well, all her girls were hos, and they taught me how to walk in high-heeled shoes and wear makeup when I was six. But I ain't livin' that life. I'd rather die."

"Yeah, I tried to die once. I took a bunch of pills, but it didn't work. "

"Me too."

Erika continued, "I had a bad relationship. . . . Well, maybe it wasn't really bad, just not quite right." She looked up shyly at us, catching our eyes to see if she should proceed. We nodded. Her eyes were soft for a moment, kind of sad, and then the sadness disappeared and she grinned at another girl. "Yeah,

I was prostitutin' then, you know, and my boyfriend would get all nosy and into my business. He came home this one night and wanted to fuck me, but, you know, I'd been fuckin' all day and didn't want it. He made me. He just fucked me and left." She paused, then asked, "Can that be rape?"

Evie turned to us, her deep brown eyes wide and round. "I'm gonna fuck them up before they do me," she said. "I ain't putting up with no shit. I'll cheat, leave, pistol-whip them bastards, whatever. I ain't got no man—and hey, I'm the only one here who doesn't have anyone to come visit. No dude, no family. The way I see it is that I do what I got to do—I don't fuckin' care if it hurts you."

The loneliness exploded on her face, along with defiance, rage, pain, and lies and stories to cover up shame and pain and real stories too horrible to tell.

We began to steer the discussion toward the ways people learn to survive. All of them had learned to survive by covering years of woundedness. They were only fifteen, fourteen, or sixteen, yet some were in jail for murder, assault, robbery, or prostitution, applying survival mechanisms to years of childhood pain. Yet they were still just little girls with vulnerability in their eyes that they were too quick to hide, with long-unexpressed pain, looking for a safe place to lay it down and go forward. But the road isn't clear. It's challenging to expose wounds when those you have trusted became unsafe.

As grown women, we still know this too well. There are some wounds from childhood that never go away. We've learned to work with them, but it has not been easy. These girls are just starting out on that journey, and we want to give them the best set of tools and resources as they commence. It will be a bumpy road indeed.

Sometimes it can seem as if the old wounds will never heal, and a woman may believe that she can take no more. She thinks that there is no hope to be found, and that the way forward is too exhausting. Those points are dangerous intersections in a woman's or a girl's life, for without proper support, she may conclude that her life is not worth living. The next story is about such a woman. It is a story of despair, but it could easily have been a story of hope instead.

She was a grown woman whose heart had been disregarded too many times, and her value steadily diminished as her despair continued to grow. She really did not see a way out. Those years she'd lived in abusive relationships added up, and the subsequent years of living without love, or with off-and-on men who lied, cheated, laughed at her, and mocked her heart—they took their toll, too. So great was her sadness that she thought her only choice was to leave. There seemed to be no way to fix her immense pain anymore.

Dressed in her favorite pajamas and ready for sleep that didn't seem possible, she got in her old car at 3:00 a.m. and drove to the bridge. There was a history there; at this bridge above the almost-dead river, she had a history of whispering prayers and throwing rose petals and creating hope. On this night, though, hope was elusive and noncompliant. At the hour of the morning when only the most despairing are awake, she parked her car and walked through the early-morning mist to the bridge.

The high-pitched moan of the sad sirens of fire trucks and the screeching of police tires were the dominant sounds of the city night. The human sounds of running insomniacs and commuters leaving before sunrise were about her but didn't seem quite real. How had she gotten to this place on the bridge, on this night?

She kicked off her flip-flops and climbed the rail. *Damn*, she thought, *it would be better if the streetlights were less glaring—no darkness to see the depths of the water*. As the annoying glow blinded her, impossible thoughts of survival passed momentarily before her. In her forty-seventh year, tired of waiting, tired of struggle, weary of being disappointed, she imagined herself off the bridge and levitating momentarily through the air, before she reached the waters that would carry her spirit to the sea that she loved. Such was her disappointment and despair that she could see no other way out of the perpetual pain.

A bit hesitantly, barefoot, one small foot and then the other, she climbed the rail until she could hang her torso over the edge and see the blackness of the water beneath her. No one came or saw, and deep inside she knew it would be only a momentary loss for most. Slightly embarrassed that she would stoop to this interior pain, she tried to pretend that she was not really jumping—"just practicing," she would tell someone if they stopped. But, good God, if they stopped, she would be hospitalized! No, that wouldn't work at all—loss of dignity was even worse than death. *Forgotten* was a possibility that occurred to her, too, but that had a less lasting effect.

Why hadn't she written a suicide note? What would her children think? They were pretty much grown and didn't need her, though, and someone would take care of her dogs, as lovable as they were.

Another step up on the rail, and then just one leg over, onto a perch on the edge of possibility and time. She was almost there. What she remembered was the suicidal man from her old town and how he had practiced killing himself by driving in his truck to remote places for several nights with his shotgun in his lap, until he gained the courage and the will to pull the trigger. Did he regret it? She always wondered and was obviously unable to ask. He had a wife who had made him go to therapy, even though he had not talked there. But she cared, and she went to the therapy appointments after he was gone.

What soul-weary place brings a person to this lonely point? Many things go into a death. It is not a moment in time but a series of events that is unknown to the time that we abide in by day. It is the time of darkness and turning and promises spoken softly and infinite chanting that does not exist in this world, channeled visions on mountaintops inside old cars with sake, an old man, and two girls captured by his magic. It is the language of unfulfilled dreams and all the goals someone once held for you melted into ethereal space. It is no longer human, no longer solid. In the breathing of the dying, the spirit fights its way from the body. In the breathing of suicide, one's heart races with the anticipation of flight.

She moved ever slowly. She could not see the moon, her favorite. Was it really just yesterday that she had said, "These are things that make life magnificent—the moon and the trees"?

That was yesterday, though. Tonight she could not see the moon to say good-bye. One more leg over the rail, and with the gentleness of the morning breeze, her nightgown consumed by the air, she set sail on the winds.

CHAPTER 6

THE HUNGER

So we dug in, stayed put, eating the weeds that grew on the shore, bringing down gulls with crude arrows or stones, spearing the odd fish from the rocks, accepting whatever sea-life was thrown at our feet by the storm.

My words had frightened the men. But fear doesn't last, and hunger has first call on the brain. . . . Once the appetite starts to talk it's only a matter of time.

—The Odyssey: A Dramatic Retelling of
Homer's Epic, by Simon Armitage

One of the most common themes of our discussions with young women who have been sexually exploited is the theme of hunger for love. It isn't necessarily stated outright, and sometimes it is not stated at all; however, it does show up in numerous ways and countless conversations about family and significant relationships. It shows up in how the girls describe themselves and their sense of worth. It shows up masked sometimes by toughness, pain, and numbness or covered by drugs, alcohol, and other addictions or self-destructive behaviors. The sense of hunger, whether it is physical or metaphoric, is shared by all human beings. The difference in the metaphoric hunger experienced by sexually exploited young women or adult women survivors lies in the forms that the hunger takes on. Arguably, all children who grow up without the necessary constructs of safety, security, belonging, and love are at risk for being metaphorically hungry for these basic human needs, and, like physical hunger, the hunger for these next-level basic needs can be thwarted, perverted, and unhealthy unless those needs are adequately fulfilled.

Abraham Maslow's well-known and much studied "Hierarchy of Needs"[42] describes a pyramid structure whose base comprises the needs that are most essential for survival—such as sleep, food, breathing, and water—and then builds to the next layer, which consists of safety needs such as security of the body, resources, health, and home. The premise of Maslow's hierarchy is that basic needs must be met in order for higher levels of needs to be met. Although his theory is linear in approach, there is much truth to be found in it. As humans, we need to have our basic needs of safety and security met in order to function well and to meet the higher needs of love, acceptance, belonging, and intimacy; then we need to experience love, acceptance, and belonging in order to meet the next order of needs, which include self-respect, esteem, confidence, achievement, and eventually more spiritual and transcendent skills.

Along with other theories of psychosocial development, Maslow's theory is helpful for this particular discussion because

---

42. Abraham Maslow, "Some Theoretical Consequences of Basic Need Gratification." *Journal of Personality*. June 1948, 402-416.

it does offer insight into how a person's development can be stunted when such basic needs are not met. We are better able to understand that within all humans comes a need for social community, love, acceptance, and family, as well as more basic needs of food, security, and resources. When any of the basic needs are not met in a young person, then a host of compensatory behaviors and strategies takes over and these strategies begin to dominate the metaphoric hunger, essentially because the original needs were simply unmet or met with trauma. The two stories that follow typify this unfortunate scenario.

He said, "Beauty is in the eyes of the beholder, and right now, I'm the holder." It was bullshit, of course, as her mother warned her, but at fourteen she thought it seemed sincere, and he was an adult. She had only dabbled in adolescent romantic yearnings— the newness of the kiss, the tugging in the heart—and it was reassuring to know that she was pretty and desirable. Something in her desperately yearned for belonging, love, acceptance, and the chance to be someone's beloved. That seemed like what all girls wanted, but something was different for her than it was for her friends. It was something that set her apart from them and made her cringe inside. It was a kind of shame of being. It was a knowledge of something that should not be known and that she could never quite put her finger on. All she did know was that she was a boat adrift and she was lost. And, being lost, she wanted to be found and cared about. Funny thing, though— when one is lost, even dangerous assistance is welcomed.

What she felt that night became a pattern. "If I give you me, then will you love me?" It morphed into other forms, too: "If I give you sex, will you keep me safe?" or "If I give you all of what you want, will you care; will you find something of treasure in me; will you stay and not leave?" All were bargains not kept.

Bad deals of the soul lead to disillusionment, sadness, torment, and the road to hell, but little girls don't know this, and big girls who never learned don't know what they don't know. Because the deals were never kept, she began to doubt her worth. Was it something in her that was intrinsically not enough to matter? Haunting voices grew to inhabit a larger space of her mind, until her own voice grew fainter and then unrecognizable. The haunting voices eventually birthed a monster who dominated her life. The monster was an ice queen who was too frozen to care and could have sex with multiple men and not remember their names. She could fake pleasure. She could pretend. She could trade sex for drugs or money or for the pretense of love. She would say good-bye to them before they left. She would run away, move, get out of town, fuck off, hit the road, Jack. The queen felt nothing, not even her breathing. But the haunting voices were starving for love unexpressed, unrequited, and unknown, and they gobbled up all that looked like food, even if it made them sick.

I pushed aside the guilt I felt for being intimate with this man. I was trying to turn my life around . . . but I really liked him, and I knew he really liked me, too—I just knew it. Everything was perfect. Slow jams played in the background; he lay back, arms above his head, enthralled (I imagined) by my beauty and my skills (whatever that meant). I closed my eyes, on top of him, and fantasized about being in love, spending my life in someone's arms—maybe his?—and being loved, safe, secure, happy. I was lost in my own thoughts, transported to another place (as was not uncommon during most stages of intimacy); I didn't notice his distraction, fidgeting, moving. Until I felt it—the cold, hard nose of the revolver at my temple, bringing me crashing back to reality.

I was dazed at first, and I froze. Opening my eyes in the dusk, I tried to search for his eyes for a reason, understanding, something. Did this dude really have a gun to my head? In the milliseconds that followed, I stayed still, motionless, even, like a fawn caught by an oncoming car in the middle of the street. Finally I found his face in the dark. His eyes were piercing, emotionless, unreadable. Then he broke into a grin. Chuckling, he returned the gun to its resting place underneath his pillow. He grabbed my waist. Obviously turned on, he resumed his rhythmic thrusting. He pulled me close and whispered in my ear, "Oh, baby girl, I'm just playing. . . . You shoulda seen your face! I would never hurt you, baby. . . . Come here, girl. . . . You feel so good to me. . . ."

At that moment, the message to my psyche was loud and clear. *Make the wrong move, and I'll kill you! Don't fuck up!* Yet in my consciousness, my reality, clouded by the soft music and the intimate sexuality, there was a sense of relief, a sense of familiarity. Here it was again, that familiar blend of pain and pleasure, love and hate. The hunger drove out the fear, and the fantasies returned: *He's so crazy; he plays too much. . . . He must really trust me to show me his fantasies, to reveal to me the hiding place for his gun. . . . I know he likes me; I just know it.*

~⊙~

Rachel Lloyd, executive director of Girls Educational & Mentoring Services (GEMS) in New York and author of *Girls Like Us*, describes the following:

"When someone has the power to take your life but doesn't, you feel grateful. It may not make logical sense. Given that most people haven't experienced someone wielding the threat of death over their heads, it can be hard to understand just how intense that type of bond can feel."[43]

This moment, as all the other moments, was a red flag missed, a clear indicator something was terribly wrong. To a broken spirit and a starving soul, it was the beginning of the end, as were all the other beginnings and all the terrible endings. Many girls describe similar experiences, times when, at the hand of a boyfriend or a pimp, they have been close to death, seen their life flash before their eyes, really wondered if they were going to make it. Funnily (or not so funnily) enough, these occurrences at the hands of someone who "loves" these girls rarely ever scare them enough to make them leave. Oftentimes the events are followed by an apology or flowers, or merely awkward laughter, and the red flags fade.

---

43. Rachel Lloyd, *Girls Like Us: Fighting for a World Where Girls Are Not for Sale* (New York: HarperCollins, 2011), 162.

The affection that follows the abuse is analogous to a tea-spoon of broth after a long fast. It is a crumb thrown out to one who is so hungry, she scarfs it down, and although she never feels satisfied, she doesn't quite know what satisfied is . . . so she feels thankful. Thankful that someone loves her enough to feed her a crumb, a morsel, a piece of bread.

The "Cycle of Violence or Abuse," as first described by Le-nore Walker, psychologist and a mother of the anti–domestic violence movement in the United States, states that by nature abuse creates dependency. The honeymoon experienced dur-ing the cycle of violence exacerbates the hunger; this cycle is learned very early on in lots of families, and it also contributes to the hunger—the "walking on eggshells" is familiar, as is the relief felt once the violence/eruption is over and the honeymoon has returned.

There are many additional forms that hunger, or longing, for love take on in a person's life that have little to do directly with love or acceptance or belonging. These dysfunctional pat-terns of compensation are much more connected with how a person deals with a lack of love, maltreatment, and/or trauma. These patterns are similar to the patterns of trauma experienced by victims of sexual assault and child sexual abuse. They are really patterns of self-abnegation, dissociation, and survival. They may function as protection for a time, but in adulthood they become albatrosses that don't allow for healthy relation-ship patterns to emerge.

These patterns take on different forms in individual lives, but in all of these patterns there is an innate desire for the benefits of healthy attachment. Looking at life stress, researchers find that people function best when they have at least one close attachment to another person. Lack of reliable support exacerbates anxious attachment behaviors.

∽⟨☙⟩∾

Hunger drives a person to extremes in behavior, previously never considered. The story of La Llorona is an old Hispanic legend that has been passed on for many generations. It serves as a cautionary tale not only about giving one's power away, but also, more intentionally, about how a woman must beware if her value and identity are defined by the man with whom she shares her life. Should he be not a man of honor but one who uses and abuses, she may very well fall prey to him. In the story of La Llorona, the woman loses herself and sacrifices her children and her life for a love that is unreciprocated. The following is one survivor's story of her experience with La Llorona in her nocturnal dreams.

∽⟨☙⟩∾

La Llorona visits me in my dreams. Tall and slender, she is strikingly beautiful. Her hair, the blackest black, cascades down her shoulders to the small of her back; her skin, the brownest olive, is smooth, flawless, even; her lips are full and pink; but her eyes . . .

Her eyes, the mirror of her soul, reveal her pain. Not all

the pain—she is too guarded for that, and some of the pain is far too deep. Her eyes don't reveal the insults cast at her as she walked the streets of her youth. She was beautiful, no doubt, but at times it felt like a curse. She didn't fit in. The boys wanted only one thing from her. The girls, filled with envy, didn't trust her. She was always alone, it seemed. Her eyes reveal her pain, but they don't reveal it all. They don't tell of the secrets locked far away in the recesses of her heart, buried so deep she wonders if they are even real. They don't tell of the times she pretended to be asleep when he came into her bedroom *por la noche*.

He told her she was a beautiful little girl, *una hermosa niña*. He caressed her so softly, he made her skin crawl. He made her promise not to tell, told her she'd better stay pretty, told her he would teach her how to please a man, told her she tasted so much better than her *mamá*, promised her he'd always love her.

Her eyes, mirrors of her soul, full of tears, try to hide the pain she felt when her mother turned away—the rejection, the anger, the jealousy she saw caught her mother's eye that made her afraid to look. "You think you are so pretty, *chica bonita*," her mother would say with a snarl. "You are damaged goods. No man will ever want you."

La Llorona, the weeping woman, wails in my dreams. She tells me her story. She moans as she tells of the time they met. She thought he was her love, *su amor*, her life, *su héroe*. He was supposed to rescue her, take her away from all the pain; he was her way out. He loved her, he said it, she believed him. They began a life together, she bore his children, she thought it would always be. Leaving her was gradual at first. He would stay out one night, maybe two. He always came back. He missed her, he said. He missed *sus hijos*, his children. He fed her crumbs, excuses, lies. Soon his visits became less frequent. Her hunger grew. Her craving began to consume her. She needed him, she thought; he was supposed to make things better. Then the rumors began, the stories around town, of his women—fancy women, rich women, extravagant, picturesque, pure women. The types of women she would never be.

She calls me to the water. I follow her in my nightgown. My feet are bare; my heart breaks to hear her cry, "Oh, my children. *Ay, hijos mios.*" Her dress, the whitest white, trails behind her like a bridal gown, her body a silhouette beneath the thin fabric. I struggle to keep up. The bulrushes are high, the ground soft. She knows her way and travels much more quickly than I.

She stops at the water's edge and falls to her knees. I fall beside her. I want to hold her, pray, stroke her hair, tell her it is going to be okay, but I don't dare. Her hand, old and withered now, stretches out of her gown; her bony finger points to her heart, "*Ay, hijos mios,*" she wails. She turns slowly and looks at me. I finally meet her gaze. Her eyes, the mirrors of her soul, finally reveal her pain. The pain is too deep, the force too strong, the anger too great, the agony too intense. She reaches out her hand to me. . . .

I wake with a start! My heart is racing, breathing heavy, my hair damp with sweat. I lie in the darkness and consider the tale of La Llorona, the weeping woman. Legend has it she was beautiful and manipulative. Abandoned by the man she loved, she murdered her children. Out of grief and jealousy, she threw their bodies in the river. Ultimately, the man rejected her and she killed herself.

I consider La Llorona for hours. I consider the pain of her story, the ghost she has become. I think of so many young girls, the way they have been discarded, thrown into rivers, accused by many of seducing men; and the way they wander, almost ghostlike, searching for something they will never find. I want to tell them not to be afraid. La Llorona cries for them, she looks for them, she warns them. Maybe she is warning me, maybe she *is* me. We weep together.[44]

Hunger plays out in many ways in the lives of young people who are insecurely attached or who have experienced multiple traumas. There is no easy answer to addressing these deep needs, but we begin by listening and offering our empathy and support, as Stacey does in the following story.

"It's hard to describe the hunger," said Alisa quietly, looking down. "It's like, I know he doesn't care about me, but sometimes he's all I have." She gazed around the room, avoiding eye contact, looking intently, as if searching in the corners of the building for the answers. Her hands wrapped around each other, nails bitten, polish remaining in splashes—neon colors. "When he says he loves me, I believe him, you know."

She looked up. I nodded. I did know. I knew the feeling, the longing, the hunger.

---

44. "The Spirit of La Llorona," http://www.lallorona.com/La_index.html.

"One time," she said, a slight smile turning up the corners of her mouth, her dimple beginning to peer out from the curve in her cheek, "after he dropped me off, I thought he wasn't coming back. I kept looking outside to check. It was the worst feeling ever, like he had abandoned me. I forgot all about the crazy stuff he had me doin'. I was so scared he was gonna find somebody else. I didn't want to be replaced. I needed him to love me like I needed air to breathe. When we were apart, I held my breath . . . literally!" She paused. "He's become my comfort zone," she said, looking at me again.

She was beautiful, dimples so big they erupted even without a smile. Her eyes were watery, like dark, still, tropical pools. A large scar furrowed across her eyebrow and spoke of many more experiences she still had to share. "I used to laugh at them hos talking about 'dude be handcuffin'. . . .' Now I get it. It's like I'm in prison but there are no bars. I have handcuffs on, but when I check, nothing is around my wrist." She picked at a hangnail, bringing her hands to her mouth to nibble at her skin. "The thought of being alone was worse than being out there! At least out there I had him, you know? I knew I could make him happy. He needed me." Her eyes filled with tears, like ancient wells from which her ancestors had drawn water. "I think I feel like he's all I can get, even though I know it isn't true. Bad or good, this life is what I deserve. . . . I don't think I can do it without him, Ms. Stacey. I'ma just be real witchu: he's the only one who's really been there for me, you feel me?"

Yeah, I thought, *I feel you*—not in a therapist-ish, feeling-the-need-to-validate kind of way, but in a true, deep *I have felt that pain and I know the feeling of that hunger* kind of way. I nodded and smiled.

In the same way Alisa was feeling the hunger, I was enduring my own fight. Smack dab in the middle of a divorce, I was learning my own strength, discovering my own boundaries. Alisa longed to be loved, accepted, valued. Rejection meant you were unworthy. I don't want to pretend the dissolution of my marriage in any way mirrors the layers of trauma experienced by children who have been commercially sexually exploited, but I, a professional, mature, "successful" woman, knew the hunger and fought the residue of childhood abuse and the long-standing pain of multiple rejections. I, too, had to fight the desire to feed my starving soul with the crumbs of limited affections. I had to learn not to consume the leftovers. I had to learn how to nourish my spirit so that I wasn't starved for attention and settling for misuse. But the learning takes a long time.

We sat for a while in the silence, presumably lost in our own thoughts: she in thoughts of him, I in thoughts of *How do I reveal to this beautiful child her worth? How do I help prevent her from enduring years of broken relationships and empty tables? How do we feed the hunger?*

The phenomenon of inmate dating is another issue that many girls and women who are survivors face. Often, after being released from the chains of exploitation, they are looking for something easy, something safe, something that satisfies their desire to be loved but does not really cause them to risk too much. For a broken woman, an inmate relationship can feel like the answer to her prayers. Many women—as we have seen in the number of wedding proposals Scott Peterson received after he was convicted of killing his wife, Lacy, and his unborn son, Conner—long for the security of a secured man, the commitment of one committed. Ironically, it feels safer somehow—not really risking being hurt, his walking out, some other woman walking in and taking her place. Women who choose to date inmates may think, *As long as I know where he is and that he is thinking of me, I am happy. And of course he is thinking of me. He tells me all the time in his letters, phone calls, Facebook posts. I am all he needs to get through this situation. He can't do it without me.*

For many of our girls, the men they love end up behind bars. These are the pimps the girls are called to testify against; the baby-daddies who, weeks before their child's birth, commit another mindless crime; the long-term boyfriends who, after they get locked up, decide they want to settle down. Then there are the women who meet their partners after they have been locked up—the Mrs. Mansons, Mrs. Petersons, and Mrs. Menendez'. They wait as long as they can, putting their lives on hold to prepare for their men's homecoming. They prepare for family visits and put together care packages. Weekend meetings and weekly letters become their crumbs. Frequent and intense, the crumbs fill them up. They are no longer starving. They are satisfied and open for the first time in a long time.

A male inmate listens; after all, he has been longing to hear a woman's voice, to drown out the testosterone-charged bellowing he has grown accustomed to. He is sincere as well. He waits for her visit, calls on schedule, prays there is no lock-down. He cherishes the ten-second embrace he is allowed at the beginning and the end of the visit. He sits across the table, shuffling cards and sorting dominoes, exchanges pleasantries with someone's wife, mother, sister. He prepares the vending-machine sandwich as though it were a delicacy, feeding her slowly, hoping her lips will touch his outstretched finger. Some touch hands on the glass and whisper into the phone, placing the receiver on a protruding belly so he can sing lullabies to his unborn child. For all, a make-believe reality has been created: *we are a family, we are normal, we are successful, soon I will be home and it will be all better.* Sadly, cultural actuality in the United States dictates that one in three black men are in prison or on parole. For many women, this has become a way of life.

For the many young people growing up without adequate sup-port and love, and for the many adults whose young-life trau-mas were never resolved, the appearance and hope of family and belonging can override the realities of a bad situation. If enough morsels of hope and the appearance of being a couple or a family are present, then it is easier to convince oneself that one's needs are actually being met. Unfortunately, this is often at the expense of the health, well-being, or feelings of self-worth of the woman who gives her best for a taste of some reciprocated love, when in actuality it is all an illusion designed to keep her in a complacent and unquestioning place and under control. Sometimes that hunger dictates and determines a woman's actions and reactions to a point where the dream becomes more authentic than the reality of the situation, as it does in the following story that Stacey shares.

One of our girls sent a text today. Her baby's dad has been arrested.

"guess whoz in jail again."

But the baby's almost here, I think, feeling instantly sorry.

"even doe we not togetha I wantd our son to meet him wen he open his eyes u know"

Yeah, I think, *that really sucks.*

"he fukd up," she says, obviously stressing, clearly upset.

I console her, reassure her—tell her to stay focused, not to get upset, she is going to be a great mom—and I mean it. Several texts later, we end our conversation and I reminisce.

I remember the years of prison letters and collect calls; I remember children visiting the penitentiary, thinking, *This is a normal life.* I don't want that for her; I don't want that for the baby. Even though she says she's not going to take her son, I know she wants him to see his father. I worry already about her and the hunger. I worry about the crumbs he may feed her. I worry about postnatal attachment and infant bonding. I worry about another boy growing up without a father. I worry about another father growing up without a son.

I pray that night about a society in which more black boys are locked up than are sent to college. I pray about parents putting aside their agendas and sacrificing for their children. I pray about girls and women who are lonely and hungry, and I pray they will find nourishment. I understand, however, that as much as I want to scare her with these details, discuss statistics with her, tell her horror stories, I must ultimately pray that she eats. I must fill her plate as much as I can and show her places where she can find "food." As Odysseus reminds us, fear doesn't last, and hunger has first call on the brain. . . . Once the appetite starts to talk, it's only a matter of time.

There are memories that haunt adult lives and that, when remembered, point to early choices and decisions that took root in the psyche as patterns of behavior. Sometimes, early decisions to listen to our wildly afraid inner voices lead to our obsessively hanging onto semblances of love at all costs. Before we can heal, we must look squarely at these patterns that took hold, and understand how they have hurt us, as well as protected us.

In the next piece, a woman tells of an experience that was imprinted upon her as a statement about her lovability and worth—an experience that occurred because she was a survivor of early sexual abuse and that also opened the doors for the continuation of traumatic events with intimate partners. This phenomenon can lead to a host of other symptoms that make up the horror that is complex trauma.

My life appeared normal and middle class to most, but underneath the surface, there was darkness that was never spoken about. Consequently, I made many choices out of hunger. One time, when I was sixteen, I walked out of a spring-concert band performance midway through, at 8:30 p.m. I finished playing a piece, packed up my instrument, and walked out during the clapping. I didn't turn back, hurried to the front of the school, my beautiful new yellow dress flying in the wind, covering my head from the rain, and waited.

Andy said he wanted to see me. He said that he would pick me up at eight thirty. He said that he wanted to see me tonight and had free time. He said that it had to be eight thirty, not later, and even though I told him that I had a concert and should not leave before it was over, he said he had an early morning the next day and needed to pick me up then and it couldn't be later. Okay, then. I was there at eight thirty. I was there at eight forty-five, nine o'clock . . . At nine fifteen, I heard the final clapping and knew the concert was over. I had been cowering under the awning of the high school to keep dry from the swirling spring rains blowing in diagonal sheets across the flatlands of farmland small towns.

I hurried to my car before the people began to trickle out. I was too frozen inside to cry, gasping for air, holding my breath—I had walked out of a concert! Yes, I had walked out of a concert because I thought that a man cared for me, and he said he loved me. This one said he loved me, so I had to go, right? I had to go.

Fortunately, I got home quickly, before my parents. I ran to my bedroom and slammed the door. Safe. I opened the window wide, put on Bruce Springsteen loud, and sobbed in the windowsill for who knows how long. I bit my left hand hard, as I always did when I felt pain. Bit my left hand to muffle the cries, to forget the tears. It was an old habit—who knows how old: focus on the pain of the bite; bite harder. Not the tears. No, never the tears. He had stood me up before. I had been stood up enough times by enough men and boys that I knew I was just fortunate if they showed up. I could usually gauge it, too. This time I had messed up.

He didn't call, either, the next day and maybe the day after—frankly, I don't remember that part. I do know that I went out with him again, and I'm sure that at some point he was apologetic, but I don't remember that, either.

Unfortunately, by the time I was sixteen, I was used to being left. I was used to fear, loneliness, not being seen for the person I was, and not being valued for myself. I didn't even know what my "self" was, really.

I knew I hungered for this one. There were so many moments worth stacking the bets of one's dreams upon. Like the time we rode his dirt bike wildly down a country road to a small pond where we made love in the mud and then dove into the cool summer waters, splashing and swimming all around. Those hot midwestern nights of skinny-dipping and diving under the waters, exploring the wonders of the exquisite form of another human. And another time, when we were high and listening to old Lou Reed tunes and the cotton curtains were blowing through the farmhouse windows, open to the outside air, no screens. I do remember those times and I thought he was God. It was those times I would forget a concert for, and those times that made me alter all plans, change directions, drop all others, do what it took to hold on and to hold out. When I was with him, for that period of time, I felt safe. It was unusual.

But Andy was no North Star. He was inconsistent and never a real "boyfriend." He used me as he needed, and I responded hungrily, like a starved animal happy for whatever he tossed my way. I had learned to accept the crumbs on the floor, and as I emerged into adulthood, they became my menu. Tidbits and morsels began to satisfy when they should not have, and they became my meals. I remained hungry, uneasy, afraid, and hunger, more often than not, had its way with me.

CHAPTER 7

THE MOTHER

"Mother" is the name for God on the lips of all children.
                    —From the movie *The Crow*

It is no secret that our entry into this world sets the stage for our journey. Until recent years, though, psychological theories did not give credence to the first days of life, the importance of early, secure attachments, or the effects of maternal absence on the infant and child. For many years, the idea of the child emerging into this world as a "blank slate" waiting to be imprinted was the dominant model of the established psychological culture. But as new theories and research emerged, it became apparent that infants did carry memories, and the theories of attachment, which we have discussed previously, gained more credibility.

In the present time, we are even more willing to acknowledge how pre-birth memories impact the infant, and although there is much dispute around when the fetus or baby's awareness begins, there is agreement that infants respond to their situations pre-birth. If this were not the case, we would not encourage mothers to sing or talk to their unborn children and to create the most positive environments for birth to occur in. We do know that entry into this world holds meaning in the life of the newly born, but this is a difficult subject, as it inevitably takes us to discussions of when life begins—which is not our focus in this book or this chapter—and to the importance of pre-birth attachment to the mother, which we will touch on in the context of early sexual and emotional trauma.

In the twentieth century, the adoption of children gained more visibility and popularity with the dominant mythology that an infant could be removed from one situation and put in another situation on the pretense that the first situation never happened. Closed adoptions, as a rewriting of an infant's history and a denial of reality, were common up through the 1970s in the United States; however, in the last quarter century, the value of open adoptions has gained more credibility as shame around having a child out of wedlock has decreased.

Regardless of the situation, tenuous beginnings affect the infant—whether the child is born to a woman ill-prepared to handle motherhood, or into a situation where the infant is jolted into a new reality without acknowledgment of his or her previous experiences of the original mother. Adoption specialist Joe Soll and others have helped us to understand the impact of adoption on infants and why the simple rewriting of history does not work. Additionally, much research on child welfare has helped people to understand that system-involved children and children born into disruptive situations are highly at risk for childhood trauma of many types. These early traumas cannot be minimized in the context of individual patterns and choices over a lifetime.

Many people who work or have worked in the sex industry experienced childhood trauma that affected their early security and sense of self. Whether because of foster care, adoption, or absent or abusive parents, children without secure beginnings often have to find ways to survive and compensate emotionally for this lack of care and love in their lives. The following story is about an adult adoptee's challenges with herself and parenting her own children.

One evening, a couple of years ago, I was lying in the bathtub, struggling over new shit that seemed like old shit and feeling sorry for myself, when my mind shifted to an old track, a well-worn groove in the road of this life. I thought bitterly of my mom.

I thought of how much anger I had held inside for her over the years and how much judgment I had felt from her. I had raged against this mother who adopted me as an infant and had wondered over the years, *Why? Why did you bother? I never seemed to be what you wanted and couldn't ever please you.* But, of course, this talk came from the child self who lives inside each of us and only feels, but doesn't know, the details.

And then I thought of the mother who gave me away at birth and chose amnesiac twilight sleep to deny my existence from my birth onward. I had raged against her, too—she who would still not meet me as an adult; she who still denied my existence to protect some part of herself, or a carefully constructed life and lie—even though things remain unresolved when they are not allowed to be expressed.

The only woman I knew as Mom was a closed book to me. When I was young, she smoked incessantly and drank continually through the evening hours. She was quiet and angry, and I don't remember any conversations of significance with her; the only conversations we did have were painful. Later, in my adulthood, she ignored me but favored my husband and adored my children. I always felt uncomfortable around her, as if she might explode, break apart, or just crumble. I walked on eggshells, placated, and learned to intuit my way around her unspoken feelings, which could dominate a room. For a long time, I tried to please her, and then I just gave up and started acting out. But she was my mom and she was the anchor of my young life.

As an adult, in good moments, I saw her as an insecure woman who hid her fears behind drinking and a difficult demeanor. Like a porcupine, she was always on the verge of sending out an arrow that wounded, though now, I believe, as with a porcupine, this was her protection. Unfortunately, her protection wounded me. Sitting with her arms wrapped tightly around her and her legs intertwined, body facing slightly away, she would glance slightly over her shoulder, not really making eye contact, when she spoke to me. I avoided her eyes as well. I could interpret this as rejection or I could interpret this as fear. In early years, I chose the former, and as I grew older, I believed the latter to be true.

I learned early the importance of being strong, avoiding painful feelings, and finding hiding places in my psyche.

I learned to ignore and deny the shards of broken glass in my heart and rely on the ice in my veins. These means of coping served as great protections for a time but also left their marks. I needed a kind of mothering that I did not receive.

This is the case for many women—perhaps even for my mothers. My mother who raised me taught me to judge myself harshly because possibly she was judged harshly herself. That is probably why she lived her life as a non-recovering alcoholic. Perhaps she did not feel close to her mother. Perhaps my grandmother judged my mother harshly, too. Perhaps my grandmother felt judged by her mother as well.

It is probable that the mother I was born to felt judged by her family or culture, and that was why she denied the reality of me. Perhaps her pain and fear outweighed her love for the child she carried in her womb. Maybe she froze up inside, too, and her heart inhabited the same shards of broken glass and ice as my own. And on it goes. . . .

These are the clues that hold the secrets of unspoken rage and forgiveness. These are the clues to a bigger mystery—a mystery more than personal but also cultural in some way. The numerous stories of women's lives that I have heard over the years are scattered with stories of the effects of the mother—some healing, some tragic, but always with an impact. The most broken-spirited women seem to have been the least mothered or protected as young women. The tenuousness of early mothering or lack of mothering creates a deficit in the structure of the psyche. Consequently, I have noticed that some women who have endured horrific events in their lives, but who have had strong, sustaining mothers, often learn to heal more quickly and effectively.

My mother wounds have felt primitive, like an unexpressed scream, so ancient to me as to have existed before my first breath. They created a fear in me that has plagued my life to such an extent that, when my own children were born, I was concerned that I might not be able to love them or care for them adequately. For both of them, but in different ways, I felt very little in the beginning besides fear. I did not want to hurt them in any way, but I was terrified that I would. I did so want to love them but was equally afraid of their vulnerability and dependency. I was also afraid of feeling love for them. Off and on and to varying degrees, I suffered from severe anxiety and panic disorder for a good deal of their childhoods. My fears were completely irrational, but when they snuck up on me, they immobilized me, as panic so often does. I was a conscientious and good mother on the outside, but it was under my skin where the terror reigned. There were years when I could not drive out of town, I didn't take public transportation of any type for over five years, didn't fly in an airplane for ten years, couldn't even go grocery shopping alone. I traded old phobias for new ones; when I finally got over the driving phobia, then I developed intense stage fright. When I mastered that phobia, then a new phobia would take hold. This went on for many years. But the most horrible fear was the one that I was not fit to care for my children and would somehow injure them.

Eventually, and through much work, effort, and acceptance, I was able to find healing. Panic disorder can be remedied through knowledge and understanding of and compassion for oneself. Like so many things, it, too, can be overcome, and greater patience and empathy can emerge as a result. Fear has many old and new forms, but it has surely been a steady dance partner. I am still learning that it is not my enemy.

~~~

There are numerous reasons for maternal absenteeism. Sometimes—because of divorce, failed custody battles, or maternal abandonment—children are raised without stable mother figures. In other circumstances, because of drug use, alcohol abuse, or mental illness, mothers are unavailable and unable to give their children the love and support they need. There are an estimated 1.5 million runaway/thrown-away children on U.S. streets, and over six hundred thousand children in foster-care placements nationally. Of course, the number of children growing up without a secure attachment to their mother is almost impossible to measure; thus, an immeasurable number of children in the United States are growing up with fear, doubt, and insecurity.

Other familiar dance partners waltz in and out of our lives when we grow up without a secure attachment to our mothers. Fear and anxiety, feelings of being an outsider, unresolved grief and anger, feelings of unworthiness, angst about our own mothering, inability to trust, and ongoing relationship insecurities leap and turn across our stage, with no concern for our response. Whether we engage or not, they linger in the shadows, waiting for us to invite them in; in some cases, they dance alongside us, keeping step with our choreography and waiting for the right moment to appear.

The dance is tiring. But once understood, it ties women

together, unites the struggle, increases the awareness of each other's brokenness.

The mother wounds were, as expected, a constant theme among our group of girls:

"My mother is bipolar. We are fine until she goes bad; then all I can do is get the hell up out of there. I usually end up leaving and call my pimp 'cause I don't have anywhere else to go!"

"Me and my mom fight all the time; she always choosing niggas over me! I'm tired of it. Now she knows how it feels—I choose my nigga over her."

"My mother is soooo cute. She's like my little baby. I need to get home so I can take care of her."

"I'm 'bout to have a baby, and I'm scared as shit. I just know I wanna be a better parent than I had."

"I don't even know my mother. I've been in foster care since I was a baby. Who the fuck does that? How do you choose drugs over your kids?"

Girls Like Us author Rachel Lloyd agrees that "for many sexually exploited girls, [the mother] relationship has been the one that has caused the most pain and left the deepest scars. It took me a long time to understand how impacted I'd been not just by my biological father's abandonment and my two stepfathers' abuse but by my mother and how difficult it had been to always come second in her life to a man, to a bottle."[45]

As Bruce Perry describes in his work on attachment and child trauma, "many researchers and clinicians feel that the maternal-child attachment provides the working framework for all subsequent relationships that the child will develop. A solid and healthy attachment with a primary caretaker appears

45. Lloyd, *Girls Like Us,* (New York: HarperCollins), 59.

to be associated with a high probability of healthy relationships with others, while poor attachment with the mother or primary caretaker appears to be associated with a host of emotional and behavioral problems later in life."[46]

Also of importance is a mother's impact on the prepubescent and pubescent development of a young woman. "The brain systems responsible for healthy emotional relationships will not develop in an optimal way without the right kinds of experiences at the *right times* in life," Perry states.[47] A mother (or appropriate caretaker) truly guides a young woman through feminism and femininity, confidence and competence, security and insecurities. When that mother does not fulfill this role as physical nurturer, spiritual guide, emotional barometer, or educational mentor, her absence (physical or emotional) or incompetence intrinsically impairs that child's sense of belonging. A teen or young woman judges her worth and place in this world based, in large part, on the stability and security of her mother. As Lloyd says, "Your mother is the one person who is 'supposed' to love you and protect you, no matter what."[48]

When the developmental stages of healthy attachment and separation are interrupted, a young person often ends up following either the pathway of perfection or the pathway of retreat. As with adult children of alcoholics, women who grow up without the acceptance and nurturing of a mother many times strive to be perfectionists. Their identity becomes dependent on an external locus of control that requires them to be academically, physically, and relationally "perfect." These women often struggle with feelings of insecurity and incompetence, yet

46. Bruce D. Perry, "Bonding and Attachment in Malteated Children: Consequences of Emotional Neglect in Childhood," Teacher.Scholastic.com, 2011, http://teacher.scholastic.com/professional/bruceperry/bonding.htm.
47. ibid
48. Lloyd, *Girls Like Us*, (New York: HarperCollins), 55

present themselves to the world as highly successful and fully functioning. This perfectionism also comes with a heightened sense of responsibility and fear of failure. Their self-esteem so hinges on others' perception that they are oftentimes unable to silence the negative voices in their head that taunt and criticize them, reminding them constantly of their flaws. We often become highly sensitive to the social cues and body language of others, and in turn wonder incessantly why we don't quite belong and strategize constantly about what we must do to ensure that our position in society is secure. We constantly try to "read" the reaction of others to determine our worth, unable to find the confidence that resides within.

For some women, the struggle for perfection is too laborious and pointless. They assert loudly, as did a young lady in youth detention, "What's the point? I already fucked it up, so I may as well stop trying!" This group of women consists of those who stop trying to belong and resort to compulsive behaviors, and they can be found in situations of exploitation and violence. They move to find acceptance among marginalized groups of men and women who, like them, do not belong. They just don't give a fuck! Often they cover their insecurities by escaping into unsafe practices, such as alcohol, drugs, sex, and crime. Sometimes they are so busy surviving that they miss important cues and instead seek love and recognition from those who are unworthy or unreliable.

Frequently, women learn they cannot fully function in one paradigm or the other. We learn a dance, vacillating between perfectionism and escape, retreat and attack. We learn how to adapt and adjust and never really reveal ourselves. We attempt to maintain control of our situation by becoming who we are "supposed" to be. We learn how to play this identity game while the core of our being remains hidden and afraid. It is in the arms of our mother, our primary caretaker, that we find the security and safety to be our selves. If this security is missing, then we learn to suffer. We discover our identity, and we acknowledge, even as infants, *We do exist!*

In her chapter on the story of the "ugly duckling" in *Women Who Run with the Wolves*, Clarissa Pinkola Estes states that "when a woman has a collapsing mother construct within her psyche and/or her culture, she is wobbly about her worth. She may feel that the choices between fulfilling outer demands and the demands of her soul are life and death issues. . . . If a woman has a collapsing mother, she must refuse to become one to herself also."[49]

People say it is the father who often gives us our inspiration for how we view God. Maybe, but perhaps equally, or more so, it is the mother. Mother is who we need in order to survive, and we learn this at a very early age. If Mother is not responsive, not available, or unable to protect, then a child does what it must to survive. Author, speaker, spiritual teacher, and television personality Iyanla Vanzant agrees: "Fathers show us how to survive, mothers teach us how to flourish. The mother must teach, nurture, guide, and provide the spiritual support system that the soul requires to unfold. When a child does not have a mother, some portion of the mind, the soul, and the life of the child remains in a constant state of yearning and want. . . . Only a mother can bring forth the grace, mercy, beauty, and gentleness of the spirit, the spirit of God."[50]

---

49. Clarissa Pinkola Estes, *Women Who Run with the Wolves* (New York: Ballantine Books, 2003), 176.
50 Iyanla Vanzant, *Yesterday I Cried: Celebrating the Lessons of Loving and Living* (New York: Mass Market Paperback, 1998), 162.

Sadly, this yearning and want often creates in young women a desire to have children themselves, to satisfy a need to belong, be loved, and be needed. Some teens unconsciously assume they can fix themselves and make things right by having a baby, believing that this will balance the measure of wrong that has been dealt them, and that through the mothering experience they will heal their own traumatic wounds. Unfortunately, this rarely works.

Both of us have experienced and lived this path. We were both single mothers in our teen years and experienced the challenges of caring for a child before we knew how to care for ourselves. We have known all too well that if the original wound is not adequately acknowledged and healed, another generation of broken children will soon be preparing to continue the cycle with their own families.

Long ago, we committed, in our hearts, to break this cycle. We determined we would do better with our children. They would not go through the things we had to go through, endure the things we endured. In the depth of the night, curled up in a ball, alone and afraid, we pledged, *We will be different!*

The next story is about such a commitment.

As I sit on the couch with my daughters—teens blossoming into young women—the physical contact is abundant. They touch each other, finger to cheek, head to shoulder, hand to hair; they touch me, poke, lie, sprawl. They touch their little sister; their laps, barely big enough to hold her, spread sufficiently enough to engulf the squirming six-year-old. Estrogen abounds, and yet there is no stereotypical quarreling (at least not today). This time, there is nurturing and comfort and peace. I am thankful and full of joy. I silence any voice inside me that screams, *Stop touching me!* and push aside any longing for a little personal space. I return touch. I caress, I embrace, I hold.

The healing that has occurred in my own life has allowed me to push past the barriers and fears surrounding touch and intimacy, at any rate with my children. I think, at least on this day, that in itself is a miraculous, exquisite, incomparable wonder. It hasn't always been this comfortable. I didn't catch it with my eldest—my son came second, and being male may have made it a little different—but when my third daughter turned five, the struggle began again. Her physical touch began to make me feel uncomfortable, uneasy, unsure. I began to pull away, afraid of her advances, which all of a sudden seemed sexual, sensual, undesirably inappropriate. I had done the same with her big sister—I was sure of it. But how could a five-year-old be a sexual object? How could seemingly innocent handstands, cartwheels, and cries for cuddles be seductive?

I had five children, three under five. The youngest two required so much of my time, my single-mom time, my sparse, precious time. I intellectually and intuitively knew that touch was a way I as a mother could bond with and express love to my children. I loved them with my entire being, and yet the physicality of my own child disturbed me—how could this be? How could I, her mother, the one who loved her more than life itself, interpret her touch this way? What was wrong with me?

One day, after soul searching and quiet meditative screams, I am struck by the simplicity of the answer. The age of five was the age I was sexually assaulted, the age I became a sexual being, the age I was no longer innocent, likely the age I no longer asked for or received positive physical touch. I was uncomfortable because beyond the age of five, I didn't know how to receive or give healthy, positive, loving touch. Beyond the age of five, every meaningful physical contact I remembered was of a sexual nature. So back I went again—time to do some more work; time to take another step on this never-ending journey toward healing.

How does a woman who hasn't experienced positive physical touch learn how to touch her children? How does a mother who has never been mothered learn how to mother? How many women, I wonder, have struggled with these feelings of insecurity and shame? How do I ensure my own children feel the love and affection of their mother (and their father) so they don't grow up as starved for physical attention as I was? As Estes describes in the aforementioned story about the "ugly duckling": "By far, the most common kind of fragile mother is the unmothered mother. . . . There are no two ways about it: a mother must be mothered in mothering her own offspring. Though a woman has an unalienable spiritual and physical bond with her offspring, in the world of the instinctual Wild Woman, she does not just suddenly become a fully formed temporal mother all by herself."[51]

No wonder, amid all this brokenness, a society in search of a victim never struggles to find an appropriately hungry, lonely child; no wonder a teen, broken by her motherlessness and unfamiliar with the healthy touch of a father, becomes such an easy target for a pimp or predator, who has likely been victim-

51. Estes, *Women Who Run*, 177.

ized in his own way and experienced his own motherlessness and hunger. . . .

And the cycle continues.

Of course, there are also stories of hope. There are adults who, involved with the system as children through no fault of their own, parent their children successfully in homes filled with safety, love, joy, and laughter. There are women who, in spite of absent or unavailable mothers, had their mothering needs met among cohorts of girlfriends, healthy women's ministries, sisters, and relationships with extended family. There are survivors of sexual abuse and/or exploitation who, after they are sufficiently far along in their healing journey, reach back to mother, mentor, and love young people in situations all too familiar. Slowly, child by child and woman by woman, cycles of loneliness, fear, anxiety, and violence are being broken all over the United States.

Oftentimes, upon hearing about the issue of child sexual exploitation in our communities, women are hungry to get involved. I say to these women: help a mother; be a mother to a mother. Come alongside women in your community who may be struggling through their identity as new (or seasoned) mothers. They may need food, time, support, a cup of coffee, an opportunity to chat. They may be in college, in church or synagogue, at your workplace, on the street. In a world where every child deserves a parent, every parent deserves a mentor! Through these informal networks of friendship and community, hope and empathy grow. Adult children develop networks of love and support that provide a safety net not only for them but for their children. Adult children build relationships with their adult mothers. For our children we find, or create, a home.

Our bodies remember our early traumas and pain. These beginnings that we endure are real and important. The good news is that life is ever evolving, not on a linear path of time but in a spiral of possibility. We have the capacity to work with old pain, trauma, stored memories, and fears, and, through acknowledgment and healing work, we can address those secrets we thought would kill us. In later chapters, we will explore some of these healing modalities and possibilities. In the end, we have the ability to free ourselves if we face ourselves with grace and compassion. In the end, perhaps we learn to mother ourselves and consequently better mother our children, and our children, in turn, keep that cycle going forward by mothering themselves and teaching their children the same. Perhaps eventually we find the ability to forgive ourselves and our mothers.

This journey to healing oneself is not easy or for the faint of heart, though. For those who have experienced insecure beginnings and attachments, it is often fraught with pitfalls and challenges that would not necessarily be a problem for those who have had more secure beginnings. Sometimes it seems as if we cannot survive another day, and as if those early deficiencies define our fate. This next story is one that demonstrates that we can overcome and move boldly forward, despite our fears.

She went to Greece by herself and rode a horse for 128 miles across rugged terrain on the Pelion Peninsula with a group of four other people whom she had never met before. She got food poisoning on her flight from San Francisco to London and became violently ill. Not only was she flying to a foreign country alone to ride on horseback through the mountains for a week, but she had to figure out how to get well before she boarded her flight to Athens.

Vomiting as discreetly as possible upon landing in London and in multiple public restrooms, she made her way through the airport and, knowing that she could not board her connecting flight, determined all the necessary next steps. It was an ordeal, and she was alone. But she had learned over the years how to take care of herself, and so, very, very calmly, she made her way to a lovely and comfortable, albeit overpriced, hotel room at the Heathrow Hilton, slept for twenty-four hours, and got well again. This is the same woman who could not drive across a small town in Iowa ten years prior without extreme fear. This is a woman who at one point would not have been able to afford a hotel room in London. Life can change us for the stronger. We can and do overcome.

When she finally got to Athens, she had no layover time left and was greeted at the airport by her guide and the others. They headed off to the countryside in a jeep. When they arrived at their destination in the late afternoon, they were introduced to the horses. Her horse for the journey was a seventeen-year-old mare named Roxanne. The guide instinctively connected his horses with their respective riders, and Roxanne and the woman bonded from the first moment.

Roxanne was a "rescue horse" who had been badly abused as a young mare and fostered by the guide. When her own foal was born, she did not know how to care for him. Oddly enough, Zepharellos, her son, was also being ridden on this trip, and they had become the greatest of friends as grown horses. They loved to travel in close proximity to each other, and in the evenings, when the riders put the horses up, the two waited for each other and walked off to pasture together. There they would stand, side by side, staring off at some mutually agreed-upon spot on the horizon. Heads together, as if speaking a language known only to them, manes blowing in the wind, a fierce wildness and strong centeredness surrounding them, they seemed always to be silently and intensely bonded.

In the morning, Roxanne would nuzzle the woman's face and the woman would sing to her while they were grooming and tacking the horses. Sometimes the woman even sang as they rode, cantered, trotted, or just walked together for miles. Over the course of the week, the woman grew to love the mare. Roxanne had never been able to nurse Zepharellos; she had simply refused and turned away. Roxanne's previous abuse prevented her from caring for her offspring, and he had been nurtured instead by a surrogate mare. The guide had been patient with the horse, though, fostered her and worked with her over the years to trust humans, and eventually she had healed enough to connect with her offspring, too. Perhaps the guide possessed some sort of special "horse power," but his patience, his care, and his love had healed this mare.

There was a lesson in this for the woman. Roxanne and Zepharellos clearly had a bond of love that transcended the pain of their past. This is possible for people, too. Mothered adequately in the beginning or not, we believe healing is a feasible journey for us all. Perhaps, as author Tom Robbins once wrote, "It's never too late to have a happy childhood."[52]

52. Retrieved from: http://www.goodreads.com/quotes/53327-it-s-never-too-late-to-have-a-happy-childhood

CHAPTER 8

THE OUTSIDER

It is no measure of health to be well adjusted to a profoundly sick society.

—Jiddu Krishnamurti

Stacey's dark eyes looked up from her coffee, and she laughed. "The Island of Misfit Toys—I remember that, too! That's just too funny."

We were remembering the animated Christmas TV special *Rudolph the Red-Nosed Reindeer*, and the story of how the dejected and rejected character of Rudolph runs away after being bullied and mocked by his peers. He runs away from his family and home and sets forward into the world with Kirby the elf, who wants to be a dentist. They encounter a dangerous snowman and inclement weather and have many other adventures before they land on the Island of Misfit Toys, where they bond with others who, like them, are outsiders.

"It's such a great metaphor," Stacey said. "After all, that's how it really is when you don't feel that you belong anywhere in particular and have no firm sense of family connection—kind of like the kids we once were, and the kids we've known and worked with over the years."

It was true. We had identified with Rudolph and the other misfits when we were children, and now, as adults, we could laugh, but the memory was still clear and present. We knew the Island of Misfit Toys as a place of comfort and refuge. We remembered thinking that if there were truly a place like the Island of Misfit Toys, that place was our real and only home.

The story of Rudolph and the elf named Kirby ends happily. They are found and embraced by their original community, who have learned, because of Rudolph and Kirby's absence, the importance of accepting those different from them. Even Santa Claus is remorseful about his lack of solidarity with the misfits, and he pledges to go and rescue all of the misfit toys from the island and find them homes with loving families. It's a great story, really. But it's just a story and not how the world works.

Until we find each other, we are alone.[53]

The insider/outsider game is a game of power. The insider usually holds that power, while the outsider seeks, manipulates, or rebels against it. From an early age, children decide who will play on what team, and in early childhood we begin to know which ones will be picked for the team and which ones will sit on the sidelines and act invisible. Some people have the opportunity to play on both teams; not really insiders or

---

53 Adrienne Rich, "Hunger," in *The Fact of a Doorframe* (New York: W. W. Norton & Co., 1984), 232.

outsiders, they maneuver back and forth between the world of chosen and forgotten, occasionally picked and the next time ostracized. These are the ones who understand the complications inherent in little white lies about the reasons they were not invited to the party and the self-blame that often accompanies that bleak feeling. This worldview teaches hyper-vigilance because otherwise no one would ever know if she was in or out, and thus would have to be constantly on guard and preparing for the worst. In this world, there is no sense of safe ground to stand on. Just as Emily Dickinson wrote many years ago:

I'm nobody! Who are you?
Are you nobody, too?
Then there's a pair of us—don't tell!
They'd banish us, you know.[54]

The ones who have always felt on the outside might eventually find more comfort in their situation than folks who have had ambivalent experiences. The ones who have always seen themselves on the outside might find more creative means of channeling their outsider status through rebellion, revolt, anger, or art forms and other means of using sensitivity gained to enhance their lives.

Children who grow up in homes where there is not a solid structure of guidance and support might find themselves in any of the previously described situations, but most of the children and youth whom we have worked with in foster care and runaway/homeless youth systems have seen themselves either as outsiders or as fortunate ones who could tentatively dance between

---

54 Emily Dickinson, "I'm Nobody! Who Are You?" in *The Poems of Emily Dickinson*, Ralph W. Franklin, ed., (Cambridge, MA: The Belknap Press of Harvard University Press).

both worlds with a lot of grace and much hidden discomfort. The youth from these systems and youth from broken or absent family structures have in common the lack of external supports necessary to build a firm foundation. Without a solid foundation of support, they find it exponentially more difficult to deal with issues of bullying and shunning and with all of the things that come with outsider status.

Youth who identify as outsiders and who are physically or sexually abused have another layer to compound their feelings. They may have additional shame that enhances their lack of safety and causes them to be drawn to unsafe situations that might at first appear friendly and welcoming. When caring figures throughout life have been unsafe or inconsistent at best, then a child learns to try to get what she needs through other means. There is always a hope that the next caring adult or the next intimate partner will give them the love that these figures promise. Yet such situations only create perpetual outsiders who know no other way than one that is ultimately harmful to them, as the next story, from an adult survivor of child sexual abuse, illustrates.

"I never felt like I belonged," she states. "I thought it was just me; I thought it was because I was a single mother. I figured it was because I was not really middle class, not really working class; I didn't really fit in socioeconomically. . . . I never fit in. You don't really know how to fit in, you know? I always battle with the feeling that I'm not quite good enough to be here. It wasn't until I got much older I realized this was a gift and I was here for such a time as this. How many people feel like misfits? How many women feel like they are not quite good enough to be in the 'cool girls' club? It is liberating to stop trying, to realize I am an outsider and that's okay! To realize I do not have to conform to society's demands of me is a powerful thing. . . . I now can give voice to what thousands of other women are feeling."

Against the backdrop of the American dream, our society—both those who have "made it" and those who are pulling themselves up by their bootstraps—often minimizes socioeconomic differences. Growing up poor or with other secrets that create shame can exacerbate the feeling of outsider status among women who are now seen as "professional." Some women (and men) capitalize on their past by sensationalizing their story, readily sharing the struggles they may have endured both as inspiration for others and as a cushion for the inevitable mistakes their audiences might make. As a society and country, we want to hear stories of people overcoming broken homes, gangs, teenage pregnancies, extreme poverty, prostitution, etc. We want to hear stories of people who turn their lives around. But we also want to hear stories of how outsiders eventually conformed to that same dominant culture that established them as outsiders to begin with.

For many of us, however, our past is a very real part of our present. Even though we have displayed great resilience and overcome many obstacles to get where we are, we still fight the very real feeling of wondering if we are in fact an accepted part of this new world. In the helping profession, "outsider" can describe feelings someone may have about not fitting in, but it also describes feelings many have about the people we serve: "those people," "those kids," "those families." Until we develop true empathy about the circumstances of another, we will not fully enter into the community of healing. Until we develop true empathy, we will not be able to see our interconnectedness with others. None of us chooses the family or neighborhood we are born into and raised in, but these circumstances have a significant impact on the trajectory of our lives.

According to teacher and researcher Eric Jensen, poverty is complex, involving risk factors that affect children and adults in myriad ways. "The four primary risk factors afflicting families living in poverty are: emotional and social challenges; acute and chronic stressors; cognitive lags; health and safety issues."[55] These risk factors have played out both in the young women we have worked with over the years and in our own adult experiences. Frequently, problems associated with poverty build upon one another and make every day of life a struggle. Combine these environmental stressors with the physiological stressors of poverty and the effects of years of sexual misuse, and we find adult women functioning with chronic stress disorders and expending all of their emotional energy to keep the pieces of their lives together. Most times, we just don't quite manage.

We will discuss in the next chapter the walls and masks with which we protect ourselves, but for the purposes of this

55 Eric Jensen, *Teaching with Poverty in Mind* (Alexandria, VA: ACSD, 2009), 7.

chapter, we must mention that women often create sophisticated systems of coping in order to solicit the feeling of belonging. Illusions of control (or lack thereof) often lead people
into behaviors such as shopping, eating, or hoarding, and more
extreme behaviors, such as alcohol or drug abuse, cutting, and
sexual addictions. In the twenty-first century, phenomena such
as the Internet and social networking allow those of us who
have difficulty connecting to hide behind a persona online. We
can develop "relationships" online, we can date, chat, and visit
people's profiles, without ever really having to work on true
intimacy. We create the illusion of belonging, yet in reality we
remain on the outside, looking in.

The sirens sat, balanced on the tops of the rocks. Their soft
melodies encircled them and drifted slowly across the tops of
the blue-black waves. To many, their habitat might have seemed
treacherous, but to them, the crags and precipices had become
their home. Their voices were sweet and euphonious, sometimes
sounding like soulful jazz, other times like a classical symphon-
ic arrangement, and occasionally like a mournful love ballad.
Their tear-filled eyes smiled while they sang, most often when
singing to each other. It had become their primary means of
communication, the easiest way to describe their feelings without words. Frequently they hummed ethereal sounds—sounds
of heartbreak and loneliness and longing. They occasionally
laughed when they remembered the time before that fateful day.
When they reminisced, they sang differently, their notes high,

rhythmic, light, joyful—ancient folk songs, sounds of happier days. They had to remind each other of the time before. They needed each other to remember the days when they ran with Persephone in the meadow, the grass soft under their bare feet. The sun was warm on their bodies and turned their skin into bronzed olive. They giggled a lot; they enjoyed each other's company and the company of their mistress. Although they were her handmaidens, they felt like family. They belonged.

They sang to her then, while she picked flowers. Together they made elaborate bouquets of roses, crocuses, and lilies. They wove together irises of violet and blue, and pink larkspur, and placed the wreaths upon their heads. The music of their chorus mixing with the fragrance of the blossoms rose to the heavens as sweet worship.

As they sang, Persephone danced. Her body, athletic and strong, floated effortlessly above the grasses, spinning and twirling to the music. Her luminescent gown swirled, creating an effervescent rainbow of indescribable colors.

They didn't sing for others, though, nor did Persephone dance for her admirers. Yes, they were beautiful, but their confidence bubbled from deep within them; they did not need outside approval to be who they had been created to be. But that was before. Now they longed to belong to something, to belong to someone. Since Persephone had been taken, raped, destroyed, nothing was the same. Sent to search for her, they had welcomed their wings at the time. They had needed their ability to fly, soar high above the surface of the deep, calling for her, crying for her, seeking any sign of her. But their majestic wings and spirited flight had not been enough to find her.

When someone is missing, any unsuccessful efforts seem helpless, no sign brings comfort, until you find the one you are looking for. Even if she were found, they knew she would be different. They knew she would no longer sing; she would no longer dance. She had been through too much. All of them had been through too much. Their radiant innocence had been destroyed. Even the ships in the distance brought no solace. Every time the men came, they held out hope, but all too soon, even the men were destroyed by the violent surf. It was for the best. The men, filled with lust, wanted to feast on their sensual beauty; they wanted only to steal the sirens' song.

The cliffs became their protection. Now they sang alone, sitting on the rocks, waves crashing menacingly against their bodies. Their eyes filled with tears that they couldn't wipe away. Their golden wings wrapped tightly around their bodies. Sometimes they rocked slowly back and forth to the rhythm of their grief. They knew they couldn't go back. They would always be the outsiders. Now, they would never belong.

Some survivors of early exploitation and trauma freeze up inside and find comfort in their role as outsiders. For many of us, doing so provides the most safety. In time, some of us realize that many people would use us if we let them. Being used by another gives at least a momentary satisfaction of feeling as if we belong somewhere. If there is money involved, it can become a further indication of our worth and value. If we are going to be used, then it is better to be paid, we rationalize.

We can also taste power if we don't care. Simultaneously, in someone's arms, a person can feel cherished, even if it is an illusion. So back and forth it goes, from the "arms of belonging" to someone who pretends to care for us to the unattached, dissociative state of numbness in the beds of strangers where we believe, or hope, that we are in control.

Outsiders we are, first by chance, then often by choice. We find ourselves feeling comfortable on the periphery, taking a stand on difficult topics, challenging social norms and conventions, and going against the current. We shun acceptance at times and find solidarity with the marginalized—it is, after all, the most familiar place and the place that we have known best. Sometimes, however, we find it to be a lonely place, too.

There were times during our work travels when we'd rather have spent a Friday evening in a juvenile detention facility than anywhere on Earth. It was there, among young women—all in different places along their journeys, yet all striving to be better, closer to God or whatever spiritual entity they identified with, closer to their destinies—that we felt as if we most belonged. We all battled nightmares, divorce, panic, grief, unemployment, incarceration, anxiety, and betrayal. Yet it was there, facilitating cohesion among the girls, we knew we were wounded healers in our own ways. We were all, at the same time, broken and mended, afraid and courageous, students and teachers, and yet there, it didn't matter. Through our work with outsiders like us, we may have found what it means to fit in.

All of us can find this belonging. We can battle through doubt and disappointment and find a place where we are loved. What we must recognize is that love isn't the fairy tale we have been taught. Belonging doesn't make everything okay; being in love doesn't take away loneliness. Love is good and bad, sometimes at the same time. Our creative families sometimes mirror the Island of Misfit Toys: aunties and mamas we have inherited along the way, sisters we adopt or who adopt us. Even across miles, countries, or continents, we can find an island of safety. We must. We cannot live alone.

According to the FBI, the average age of a child's first experience with commercial sexual exploitation is thirteen; once that child is involved in prostitution, her average life expectancy is seven years.[56] Many survivors describe other girls, friends of theirs, going missing, being murdered, committing suicide, or overdosing. Thus, death becomes a far-too-common end to a hard and difficult life. Some get lucky and survive, and some even thrive—but what does that look like? Some get "rescued"—but what does that really mean?

The value of a life cannot be computed as if a person is a commodity, and yet from an early age we are taught that some lives are of more worth than others. In the industry of sex, there is tension between validating worth through uses of power and losing worth through abuses of power against us. These stories all begin in similar ways. The endings are different. Sometimes the endings are final, as the following story illustrates.

56. The Innocence Lost task force addresses child exploitation in select cities across the United States. (See http://www.justice.gov/jmd/2011summary/pdf/fy11-fbi-bud-summary.pdf.)

She was just a little girl, and now she is dead. Eleven or twelve years old, someone's daughter, alone on a playground at night, talking to boys. She was seen talking to the older boys night after night. Her breasts were larger than those of most her age; her form became womanly too early; she was playfully flirtatious, perhaps.

The boys liked it. They teased her and told her she was pretty. They all wanted to be her boyfriend. She showed up each night for the attention, carefully outfitted in a cute, short skirt or tight jeans and a shirt cut low. She probably loved the attention. Maybe she didn't get enough positive attention at home. Maybe she was always getting in trouble and yelled at for all she did wrong. Who knew that she was out night after night, dressed years beyond her age? Did anyone care? She had figured out how to turn the heads of men already, though, and some of them might even have said they cared for her.

One night, someone killed the little girl. They cut her throat and let her die. Who did this to her, and where is the outcry? Was she poor? Was she misbehaving? Does it matter when a life is lost? Some said she wasn't reported because she'd been running away. Why was she running away? What was she running from?

She was just a little girl, and someone hurt her long before she lost her life to someone who may have worked to gain her trust. Would the outcry be heard if she were a white girl, from a "good home," affluent, or a good student? Would someone tell her story then? Some might want to say that it is the same, but it is not. People assign worth to human beings each day. Our minds categorize who is important and who is not, forming convenient packages of who is worthy based on behavior, a glance, a word or two. Those who can't or don't act strongly on their own behalf are often thrown into the pile of the unworthy. Never mind if they never learned it on the lap of a mother, a kind father, or a beloved auntie; never mind if they were hurt badly. We unconsciously blame the victims more often than not. We are thankful that we are not "them."

A little girl is dead, and she is one of many who have died at the hands of someone who pretended to offer care and the possibility of trust, when instead they offered moments of terror and then death. Another girl, who will soon be only a research statistic, an unsolved crime, or a case for a child-death review team, is gone too early and tragically from life. Someone thought she had no worth and killed her. Someone made a decision that she did not matter.

We don't know what we don't know, and if we don't learn something new, then our bodies and minds remember only long-patterned responses along the track of existence. Both of us have experienced our perceived "outsider status" in numerous ways over the years, and our conditioned responses to insult and injury. Sometimes we even perceive that we are outsiders among other outsiders and, instead of finding common ground, we further alienate ourselves and huddle in our comfortable outsider camps. Sometimes we don't even notice this finely tuned survival habit. We, as so many others, have stories to fill countless books. The next story is one small example of a woman's experience in resorting to an old survival habit while traveling alone in Egypt.

The shaman said to her, "I can help you relieve that—I can help you relieve that *tension* that you feel inside. Why don't you lie down on the massage table? There, now, let me help you. Good. . . ."

It was like a piece of a strange dream. A Sunday night in Cairo, warm; curtains blowing in; incense; a dusty, hot desert night in Giza. Her driver from the hotel had stopped at a roadside shop that sold perfumes and oils. They were invited in to have tea—a lovely taste of black cumin and something akin to mint. She had been sitting on a round stool, when a man had brought out a variety of oils for all that might ail her. "Try this one for headaches or another for the female system. . . ." The smells were lovely, heavy, intoxicating. "We use this for massage," he said.

She was the only woman in the store, maybe the only woman anywhere around. It was 9:00 p.m. The older brother, in a flowing djellaba, and perhaps the owner came out from behind a curtain and insisted that she have a massage. It would be free for her; an American woman traveling needs a massage.

That is how she found herself on the table, naked and agreeing to be touched by a stranger in long robes, while the other men, including her driver, waited in the main area, speaking in Arabic, drinking tea, and smoking. Something told her that she didn't really have a choice—did she? She was afraid to say no. It was a gamble. It wouldn't be wise for her to disappear or be raped. She had family in Cairo who would notice that she was missing, and yet there were at least four men in this store—and that seemed a recipe for trouble in a patriarchal culture. She believed that she had more of an opportunity to control the situation if she was agreeable. So she took off her clothes and lay down.

He began a systematic massage of her body, kneading sweet and musky scents into her skin. He moved his hands to her groin and began to move his fingers inside her—a massage technique that he said would relieve any stress that she felt. She wanted to laugh. She wanted to cry. She wanted there to be someone who cared that she, a grown woman with children, was still in a place that held a memory of danger and aloneness. She wondered why this type of bullshit had happened to her repeatedly. She felt herself begin to freeze and then to depart from her body. It was an old habit from childhood that had once kept her safe. She vaguely remembered hearing herself protest to no avail. "Only this," he said. "I will do only this much." She was grateful for that. How stupid of her; she judged herself mercilessly. Dissociation was an old friend, and it had always been easier to disappear than to stay.

After some unknown period of time, after a reel of strange music and smells, the spell was broken and she was getting dressed. He seemed somewhat angry that she hadn't "released her tension"—she supposed he had been hoping for an orgasm of delight, instead of a disappearing woman. Maybe she had pretended a little so he would finish. Maybe she had even thanked him.

"How do you feel?" he asked.

She thought for a moment. She felt alone and sad, and wished desperately that there was a man to protect her, a man to go home to, or a man who would never have allowed her to be in this situation—again. But there never had been a protector—not her father, not her former husband, not any lover or boyfriend she had ever known, had protected her. "Like an outsider," she replied. "Always, I feel like an outsider."

"Well, that was always your choice," he replied.

The outsider phenomenon can also manifest itself in avoidant personalities, or in someone's becoming an avoider. Oftentimes survivors avoid intimate relationships. We decide, either consciously or unconsciously, that intimacy is just too difficult. This happens not only in romantic intimacy but in intimacy among close friends or family members. Being the avoidant outsider often makes us resentful, however, because much of the behavior is self-induced, fueled by a fear so great we would rather die alone than experience the disappointment and pain of rejection. As survivors, we are often hypersensitive to criticism, even if it is constructive.

Many adult women describe asking themselves repeatedly, *Why do people feel like they can talk to me any old kind of way? Why do they think it's okay to talk to me like that?* The outsider wonders these things internally because she doesn't have the closeness of trusted partners or friends to dialogue with. It's a question many of us have asked throughout our lives, as we have wondered whether the stigma and shame we feel are visible to the outside world, like a cloak identifying us as former victims, weak, unworthy.

Sadly, as we often don't have trusted friends, we can't see ourselves in the eyes of others; thus, our identification as outsiders persist and we probably continue to keep people at arm's length. When we do let people in, we may smother them with our neediness or not quite know how to maintain the boundaries of friendships. Romantic partners often shimmy our walls quite quickly. When they express love, we don't want to believe them, yet we often believe too quickly, fall for lies, cajole and convince our hearts to trust this person we don't really know yet.

We also often blur the lines of family. As our families of origin have disappointed us and proven themselves unsafe, we are always looking for somewhere to belong. Adult survivors of child sexual abuse and exploitation describe sophisticated and complex family structures that have been deliberately created to fulfill the need to belong. Survivors will often have many "sisters," "mothers," "fathers" whom they have picked up along the way. Sadly, we may adopt and involve ourselves with folks who haven't necessarily attached to us at the same level of intimacy or commitment, and that imbalance results in only more rejection, higher walls, and a greater sense of being outsiders.

On the other hand, some of us don't attach to anyone at all and prefer to "go it alone," or when we do attach, we find a way to push the other person away so that we don't risk rejection at all. Thankfully, even knowing and understanding the phenomenon of the outsider can bring us a step closer toward healing. There have been many times we, as adult women, have recognized outsider behavior in ourselves and each other. Naming it brings an awareness that in itself can be freeing.

CHAPTER 9

HIGH FORTRESSES AND MASKS

[Pain] removes the veil; it plants the flag of truth within the fortress of a rebel soul.[57]

—C. S. Lewis

Fortresses are fortified stone walls built as strongholds to protect a city, effective in keeping people out. People within the walls of the city are safe, though they give up some of their freedom in order to maintain this refuge and distance from outside forces perceived as dangerous. When we build fortresses in our hearts, we do so to keep out people who can hurt us, but, regrettably, these same walls keep out people who love us as well.

The walls we build protect us for a period of time, but at some point they begin to interfere with our ability to have our needs met or to grow as people. It is the same with the masks that we wear to hide our feelings of shame, inadequacy, or sadness. It's never easy, and sometimes not safe, to take off the mask, and it is sometimes ill advised to disarm our well-built

---

57. Retrieved from: http://www.goodreads.com/quotes/764992-no-doubt-pain-as-god-s-megaphone-is-a-terrible-instrument

fortresses. It's a process of learning whom and when to trust, and, more important, of learning how to trust ourselves.

Safety was a favorite and necessary topic of the girls we worked with in detention. In group one evening, we came fully prepared to discuss that week's subject of creating safety and learning to trust our instincts. We know that when dealing with young people in our inner cities, we sometimes cannot do anything to ensure them safety. We live in an unsafe time in unsafe communities where young people often make unsafe decisions and enhance their risk of being harmed.

Stacey opened this particular discussion by saying, "Today we are going to talk about creating safety within ourselves. For our ice-breaker, we are going to describe a place that makes us feel safe." But as soon as the words left her lips, she regretted them—she feared that the topic threatened to tear down her own walls and leave her somewhat vulnerable. She reflects, "My safe places were sacred, sophisticated strongholds built over decades to guard the divine places within me. They guarded my heart like it was hidden treasure. I had given too many the key and thus succumbed to the rape and pillage of my soul. In childhood, my places of safety varied: a fort I had made among the vines in our garden; an extravagant trail through the corn leading to a small cove in the middle of the field behind my house; a tiny opening in an alcove in my room that housed a pullout bed, among other junk, behind which I could crouch and not be seen; the window sill in my teenage bedroom, where with the curtains closed I could curl up and watch the lights of the city; the corner of my room; on the ceiling, looking down on myself as I slept. . . .

"As I kept thinking about these safe places, I remembered more: in the pages of a book, where I could be Heidi or Jo or some other heroine in the depths of my imagination; behind the globs of makeup I wore as an adolescent to cover my acne-prone skin, an orange mask that made me look quite clownish in the daylight; deep within the half shirts and miniskirts that earned me whistles of appreciation from grown men, when my self-esteem was so low that I was empowered by their admiration; on the track field, where I could run and beat the others, jumping hurdles and setting records, until practice got in the way of boys and I gave up and metaphorically also gave up winning; in the success of academics after I dropped out of high school and began using everyone's criticism to drive me forward; in motherhood, when I unconsciously vowed I would never be lonely again. . . .

"The places of protection in my life were plenteous. There are myriad ways in which I have strived to erect forts of defense around myself. Many no longer work; some never did.

"Naming these secret places was akin to revealing the treasure map to strangers. However, these girls weren't strangers; they were young women who, like we had, had safeguarded their hearts with walls of protection. We wanted to help them to strengthen their shields and become warriors. We hoped they could find within themselves places of true divinity and fortresses of truth."

◦◦◦

While we address the internal fortifications we create to protect ourselves from getting hurt, we must also acknowledge the barriers and barricades that society creates. Of these external buttresses, stigmatization is the most common and the most dangerous. Most people who have been afflicted by any type of abuse go to great lengths to mask that abuse, unable to press past the stigma and shame. Subsequently, they might not admit abuse to anyone, even to themselves.

Of all the stigmas faced by those affected by various kinds of abuse and trauma, the one surrounding sexual exploitation is the most sophisticated. We have learned, as a society, to begin to comprehend the dynamics of domestic violence; many supervision hours are devoted to coaching therapists through questions such as "Why doesn't she leave?"—although most would never say these words out in the open. In cases of child abuse, especially sexual abuse, the general public is able to generate empathy for victims and make appropriate reports to the authorities. Mandated reporters or not, callers to child-abuse hotlines demand that something be done to protect these innocent children. However, as practitioners working with youth who have experienced sexual exploitation, we still regularly hear comments such as "She just needs to stop working the streets" or "They like having sex anyway, so they may as well get paid for it" coming from the mouths of law enforcement or experienced professionals in the social services field. Many professionals seem to struggle with feeling true empathy and compassion for people, or youth (male or female), who "sell themselves" for sex. As we have mentioned in previous chapters, unless children are clearly underage and physically held in bondage and forced to prostitute, then they are often seen as at least partly responsible and criminalized by the system that is supposed to protect them. This, in itself, is a huge barrier to trust and safety.

Both society at large and individuals recovering from the sex industry internalize this stigma on a very deep level. Even when survivors are encouraged to "speak out" about their experiences and "raise awareness," many women struggle constantly with thoughts of inferiority and shame.

The following piece illustrates a story that many of us know all too well—a story that hurts us to our core and causes us to create secrets, fine masks, and very high walls around the heart.

A woman remembers:

    "Once a ho, always a ho."

    "You can't turn a ho into a housewife."

    "That chick—she'll fuck anything!"

    "You know you want it. . . ."

    "Oh, *now* you tryin' to say no? Fuck that. Come here."

    "Baby girl, we don't have to fuck—just suck my dick."

The taunts, accusations, declarations, and propositions rolled around in my mind like a marble in a pinball machine. At times the marble just rolled fairly innocuously to and fro, round and round. It became part of the noise I had grown accustomed to, one of the negative voices that spoke to me almost constantly. If I listened really hard, even though the marble continued to roll and the voices continued to drone, I could hear my heart among them, whispering sweet words of encouragement and love. At times, however, usually times of greater anxiety, the pinball machine screamed and dinged and buzzed. The lights flashed; neon colors of unbearable brightness flickered on and off. The marbles multiplied, and many rolled around at record speeds, banging and clashing into various obstacles, causing brighter lights and louder dings.

"HO."

"FUCK THAT."

"SUCK DICK."

I was certain everyone could hear. I would close my eyes and put my fingers in my ears to try to shut off the sound, but I was sure everyone could feel the movement inside my head, like loud headphones on a crowded bus; they could hear the accusations, sense the declarations. They joined the taunts with their eyes; their facial expressions and body language alerted me to the sure fact that they knew! They knew what everyone knew: I was a ho. I would always be a ho.

Most important, *I* knew. I knew with every compromising decision, every "yes" that should have been "no," every consensual/nonconsensual act, every midnight phone call or late-night knock at the door. I knew I couldn't change. I was a ho, a slut, a slag, a whore, a harlot, a siren. I was the girl who was passed around at parties. I was the one he (they) would call when they left the club: "I'ma stop by for a minute, okay?" I was who they all said I was.

I wore the mask. I didn't even try to be anything different. I smiled and flirted and manipulated. Even if that ride home ended up in a dark alley with one hand up my skirt and the other hand over my mouth, I knew—we both knew—that it was the way it was always supposed to be. I would do what I always did: hold back my tears in the car, straighten my clothes, smile as I opened the door to walk shamefully into a home where nobody cared if you were a ho or not, looking back to say, with all sincerity, "Thanks for the ride."

He'd laugh, as he (they) often did. A smile of contempt, disgust, eerie satisfaction. "Yeah."

"See you around."

I knew I'd see him around. I always did, usually with a group of his friends, half of whom had experienced the same satisfaction from me at some time or another. I would adjust my mask and walk boldly by. They were more ashamed to have been with me than I was to have been with them. I'd look at them; they'd look away. I would hear the pinball machine begin to buzz.

Game on, bitches! was the scream in my ears.

Stigmatized by their histories of sexual exploitation, gender, race, age, and class, sexually exploited young women are rarely viewed as potential or current leaders and must fight multiple layers of prejudice to be viewed outside the box of deeply ingrained stereotypes.[58] Ironically, these hard-to-find leadership opportunities are precisely the types of experiences survivors need to progress along their journey of overcoming. In light of this paradox, many women hide their histories behind a mask of success, as it is difficult to be a respected woman and have

58. Rachel Lloyd, "From Victim to Survivor, from Survivor to Leader," GEMS, 2009, http://www.gems-girls.org/WhitePaper.pdf.

a questionable past. Of course, hiding our past means that younger women, who are still struggling with their own identity, never really understand recovery is possible. Still under the auspices of losing our voice, we remain silent, passing down the masks to our daughters and granddaughters. We must have the courage to stop the cycle. We must have the courage to show our true faces.

We wear the mask that grins and lies,
It hides our cheeks and shades our eyes—
This debt we pay to human guile;
With torn and bleeding hearts we smile . . .[59]

Our masks and walls often keep us lonely and apart. One woman tells the following story, of how she came to recognize that the carefully built, protective walls she had once prized no longer served her.

She walks into the room for the first meeting of the morning and looks around. The only woman of color, again. She internally rolls her eyes. Heading straight for the coffee, she hopes a hit of caffeine will help her attitude adjust and maybe make a dent in her headache. She had a long night. Benadryl, Tylenol PM, NyQuil—nothing worked, and she was too embarrassed to go to the doctor. It would pass soon, she rationalized; this time of the year was always difficult. She had to admit, it had been much harder since he'd left. Sleeping alone was difficult.

59. Paul Laurence Dunbar, "We Wear the Mask," in *Lyrics of Lowly Life* (New York: Dodd, Mead, and Company, 1896).

She knew she would get used to it, but for now she was cold; her frozen body and her icy heart often shivered involuntarily. She cried at night when she thought the children were sleeping, afraid they would hear her and worry.

The nightmares were still frequent; last night's dream had been especially horrific. She had felt someone touching her, pulling at her hair, and clawing at her skin with cold, sharp nails, maybe even knives. She'd awoken with a start and sat up in bed. It was dark, but she sensed another being, a presence, in the corner of the room. Was it him? Had he found a way in? Was he waiting there in the shadows? She inhaled sharply and reached under her pillow for the kitchen knife. She wondered listlessly if other women kept weapons under their pillows. She grabbed the handle firmly. *Someone is gonna die tonight*, she thought. She would have to remain quiet—the children. She stayed motionless, although she was sure he had heard her move by now.

Slowly her eyes adjusted to the darkness. No one was there. She was dreaming . . . again. She left the light on for the rest of the night and of course was restless; she was sure the bags under her eyes showed her lack of sleep. The rapidly growing pimple on her forehead didn't help, either; she tried to cover it with her hair.

Looking up, she realized she must have been staring into space. They were watching her, with that subtly sympathetic look of pity and disgust. She was sure she wasn't imagining it. They thought they were better than she was. They probably were. At least they deserved to be here. She took a deep breath. Slowly adding sugar to her coffee, she calmed her heart and composed herself. She adjusted the mask she wore and walked briskly and assuredly to her seat.

"Good morning, everyone," she said assertively through her mask. She wore the mask of success and ambition, the mask of confidence. Inside she felt as she always felt, an outsider; but outside she was smiling and proud. She knew by now how to pull her shoulders back and lift her head: *don't let anyone know what you are really feeling, and most of all, don't let anyone know your past.* Then they would know who she really was!

It was exhausting. It was painful. Somehow, she knew that she must find her way out of this prison that had once been a safe place. She must find a different connection with herself and with others she could trust.

Author and psychologist Dana Jack describes the narratives of depressed women that mimic conversations described by young and adult survivors of sexual exploitation. The first-person voice, the authentic self, speaks from experience; she knows and understands; she often gives grace. The other voice, the one Jack calls Over-Eye, is decidedly patriarchal and often judgmental. It conforms to cultural and perceived expectations in order to gain approval and protect the true self.[60] Over-Eye convinces women of the masks they must wear in order to be accepted and obtain their ultimate goal of being loved. The consequence of taking the mask off is not only the risk of exposure but the fact that one could lose love. Over-Eye main-

---

60. Dana Crowley Jack, *Silencing the Self: Women and Depression* (New York: Harper-Collins, 1993), 94.

tains, "If you want anyone to love you, this is what you have to do."[61] Love, of course, is not just the intimacy between romantic partners, but the love of one's children, friends, colleagues. All love may be jeopardized if someone takes off the mask. And love, in this case, is earned and not given.

Over-Eye's patriarchal and judgmental nature is apparent in the workplace as well. Every morning, women, survivors, mothers, and others put on the mask of a superwoman and sacrifice their true sense of self to be indestructible and unconquerable in the workplace. Even woman-centered organizations seem to grapple with the competition and power struggles symptomatic of male-dominated, hierarchal bureaucracies.

In religious systems, women frequently put on the mask of submission, not quite understanding the implications it may have on the psyche. For a sexual-abuse survivor, the dichotomy of submitting to a sexual authority who is supposed to be someone who "loves you" can be extremely dangerous and potentially destructive to intimacy. Many adult women have described donning the mask of "willing sexual partner" in order to fulfill wifely responsibilities while systematically constructing a wall of dissociation in order to protect their heart and soul. Thus, many men come away from sexual encounters dissatisfied and confused, noticing the distance but not having enough understanding to comprehend their wives' or partner's experiences.

In dating it is not very different either. Culturally, women are told to be a "lady in the streets and a freak in the sheets." No wonder many of us, sexual-exploitation survivors especially, struggle with wearing the right mask at the right time. Messages from a society that demands they be sexy and desirable

61. Ibid., 100.

at all times create a falseness that is coy, instead of intimate. Walls can come down for a beloved other, and the heart can become vulnerable, but if walls stay up, then true intimacy is not possible. Sometimes, as the next story illustrates, the illusion or pretense of intimacy is a choice made while keeping one's walls intact.

She wore the mask of beauty, even at 11:30 p.m., when the phone rang. She had just gotten off the psychic hotline when he called. Her kids were in bed. This was her "moonlighting" job, and she was good at it, even though she sucked at the psychic hotline of her own life. Oh well.

It was Brandon, her latest fling, the latest broken man whom she was not really dating, just messing with at late hours, "pretending" it was more; pretending she was special. Sometimes he called when she was ironing her clothes for the next day. She'd be in her jams, all unattractive and plain, and he'd call to say, "Hey, I'm thinking of you. . . . What're you wearing?" He was hoping for a sexy answer.

Sometimes she'd say, "Why, my old sweatpants and a T-shirt"; then there'd be silence on the other end. *Hmmm.* Other times, she'd be in her old jams but she'd say, "I'm wearing barely nothing, walking around naked—you know."

He always wanted a glass of orange juice when he showed up, and he always wore a suit. He was quiet and followed her up the stairs. She was not dressed up. She was tired and it was late, but he was the closest thing she had to a boyfriend and it was a compromise she'd made with herself. He was a politician and in state government. He was important and busy. This was all that he had time for in his busy life, and she could fit him in. She was desperately lonely, and so she told herself that he cared, when really he was just a weird perv who was fucking her now and then and never even showed any sign of love or care. But she always took the time to don the mask of beauty and hospitality, even in the middle of the night.

Masks keep us safe, regardless of their intent and design. Some masks are of the beautiful, glamorous variety that puts others off and pushes away the unwanted or unworthy. Other masks are frightening and cause fear in the faces of those who look upon them. But as long as you see our mask and not our face, then you have no power over our heart, our person, or our soul. You may see a beautiful woman of confidence and little care one day, and on another day you may see someone strong, angry, and unapproachable. On the other hand, you may find the mask firmly planted, frozen in a smile or an expression that belies the feelings underneath.

All masks protect in some way and create a distance between the wearer and the viewer. Some of us live in our masks until they become our faces, and then the faces that truly belong to us are lost. Well-made masks can make you seen by many, but they can also make you invisible. Many a woman has gone invisible as she walked through the night in her mask.

Identity is shifting sand—never static, always evolving—to

the ones who wear the mask. Identity is as fashion passing. What is beyond identity cannot be accessed easily. But the wearer of the mask knows, and perhaps a few trusted ones will know, too—if all are lucky enough.

There is safety in the mask of plaster of Paris, just as there is safety in the mask of eye shadow and face paint, safety in precious red lipstick, safety in long gel nails, safety in fingers. Don't look at our hands or our veins of blue, ripe for letting blood—look at the nails, look at the lips, look at the glasses, and stay away from the eyes. There is safety in the tight black skirt, safety in the boots, and safety in the veil, safety in the cape that hides a curvy form, and safety in all the other disguises. We let you see only what you can't hurt.

She stood on the dock alone, looking out across the water. Alone and wondering where and to whom she belonged. Wondering in what tribe her origins began and whether they would find her, since she had clearly never found them.

A boat was coming from the distance. It was a pontoon boat, a party of brilliant swans floating by and waving—grand white birds with beautiful feathers, celebrating on an afternoon boat ride, leisurely enjoying the day—but still they just passed by. Like the ugly duckling of the old story, she wished she were with those gorgeous creatures. Could they be her tribe? They smiled their birdlike smiles, waved, and kept going.

A second boat followed behind, this one a pontoon boat of brilliantly hued blue herons—big birds with luminescent feathers of various shades of blue, green, and gold, so vibrant to the eye as to be stunning. They were coming to the dock, wings waving like arms to the woman. She waved back, squelching the hope rising within her. Would they stop for her? Really, was it possible that they were coming for her?

They stopped at the dock with sails and feathers unfurled and nonchalantly inquired, "Will you be coming with us? Will you join us on the boat?"

"I am not a bird," she replied. "I am a woman."

They laughed. "We are not birds, either!"

She looked surprised.

"We are blue heron women," they said, "and so are you, if you can remember. You have waited for the tribe, but the tribe is not always apparent and the walls must fall before we can be found. Your walls are crumbling, your gate is open, and you are ready, so it is time to join the fold from whence you came. Unknown and obscure, we are never what we seem. You are a blue heron woman, too."

And she lightly stepped onto the boat, taking gentle hold of the wings that offered themselves to her, now realizing her form was changing, too. Feathers formed where arms had once been, and a face turned toward the sky, where all things are possible to those who dream and learn the patience life teaches.

It wasn't the last time the herons visited her. Another time they flew angrily at her house, demanding that she come out. A flock flew repeatedly into her walls, their large bodies bouncing off as they stormed the encampment. "Come out," they demanded, "and stop hiding!"

Once a woman can shift form, she has no way to go back to the old buildings and dark-wood cabins that pretend to protect. And so she walked out the door and surrendered to the air around her—not giving in or giving up, not in acquiescence to some other person's idea of who she might be, but surrendering to possibility and the power of her heart beating. Knowing she was more than woman, more than bird—mythical, a siren, undaunted and free.

CHAPTER 10

SCARS

For women, tears are the beginning of initiation into the Scar Clan, that tribe of women of all colors, all nations, all languages, who down through the ages have lived through a great something, and yet stood proud, still proud.[62]

—Clarissa Pinkola Estes

It is easy for people to make light of scars if they have never been cut. For those of us who have endured, every mark, every scar, every dent of our soul is to be honored and cherished. Whether physical or emotional, scars can, and should, be worn with pride. Not only have we endured, we have conquered. To share our scars is to give another a glimpse into our soul, into our past, into the makeup of our being. "Nothing has a greater, longer-lasting impression upon another person than the awareness that someone has transcended suffering, has transcended circumstance, and is embodying and expressing a value that inspires and ennobles and lifts life."[63]

---

62. Estes, *Women Who Run*, 374.
63. Steven R. Covey, *The Seven Habits of Highly Effective People* (New York: Simon & Schuster, 1989), 81.

As wounded women, we are often afraid to share our scars, for fear no one may understand the depths of our pain and the extent of our suffering. We fear people may encourage us to "get over it" or "let it go." We fear our scars are marks of shame.

To share our scars, however, is to offer encouragement to women and young girls just beginning their healing journey. It is to whisper into their spirit and yell loudly, from the highest rooftop, words of love, refreshment, direction, and hope. As we move from victims to survivors to leaders, we must be transparent about the struggles and pains we still experience from time to time. We must be willing to lift up our pant legs and pull back our hair to reveal our own scars and our own difficulties.

There is no cookie-cutter formula for recovery. There is no magic surgery that can be performed on the scar tissue of the heart. The trauma endured during sexual abuse, violence, or exploitation is complex, and many of us will carry blemishes and disfiguration from it throughout our lifetimes. Many women do not even realize the complexity of their trauma. We have found, however, that there is freedom in knowing that the road to "mental health" is a long and arduous one. Most of us oscillate during "recovery," backpedaling and often regressing as issues come up and recur throughout our life cycle. Sometimes pivotal life events—such as birthdays, job losses, weddings, and deaths—trigger memories and fears that reignite the scars.

Scars were another favorite topic on group nights with our girls. We loved the conversations that ensued, and we always learned a little something new about resilience and inner strength from these discussions about this powerful yet simple metaphor. In the following story, Stacey remembers one such discussion.

"I have a scar," said Janice, lifting up her pant leg and reveal-ing a jagged white line down the side of her calf. "I was playing hide-and-seek between some sheds and cut it on a rusty nail."

"Me too," said another girl, laughing, pulling up the arm of her shirt to reveal brownish scrapes. "Wait," she said, tug-ging her navy trousers up to her knee, displaying similar marks in uneven patterns. "I fell hella hard." She giggled. "I was rid-ing my bike down the hill and fell"—she paused—"and my arm and my legs got all jacked up."

The girls laughed approvingly. They continued in a similar fashion for a few minutes, different girls sharing fond memo-ries of childhood. Their faces lit up as they recalled scooter accidents and playground calamities. Our faces lit up, too. We shared a glance at each other, both so appreciative of sharing, for a moment, a time when these kids were just kids; a time when they rode bikes and went to the park; a time when they played outside and hung out with their friends. It seemed so long ago, to them and to us.

"I have a scar," said Linda, lifting up her hair. She revealed a pink serrated scar at her hairline; it was about an inch long.

Uh-oh, I thought to myself. *Here it goes.*

"I got hit with a gun."

"I remember the first time I got hit with a gun," said an-other girl. "That shit hurt."

The first *time?* I contemplated silently.

Linda shook her head. "Hell yeah, that shit hurt."

The girls leaned forward, eager to hear the story. Their voyeuristic tendencies seemed fueled by the need to compare stories, the need to identify a commonality, to discern whether someone else had experienced the same atrocities they had been through.

There were times we felt as if we were in a veterans' support group. In a sense, we were. The post-traumatic stress disorder that victims of commercial sexual exploitation experience has been described as identical to that of twenty-year prisoners of war.

"I got outta pocket and he pointed a gun at me; then he hit me with that shit. Guess it was better than him shooting me in the face."

"I got pistol-whupped before."

"I got robbed, and my dude was mad I lost all his money. He raped me and hit me and then sent me out to make some more."

"That's fucked up," said some of the girls. Many just giggled, obviously desensitized to the horrific violence the others described.

"I bet that shit left a scar in your heart," said Paulina, a wise soul.

Ellyn snuck a glance at me. I wanted to yell, *Yes!* My excitement was brewing—maybe we were getting somewhere.

"I wonder how scars in your heart begin to heal."

"You have to bring 'em to the air," said Paulina, "like any wound. When I was little, I always wanted damn Band-Aids. My grandmother used to tell me, 'Unless that gets some air, it ain't never gonna heal.'" She smiled. "I used to cry, but she was right! If you keep that shit covered up, it ain't never gonna get better."

"I have a scar on my finger. I cut it on a can. It ain't got no feeling left."

Wow, I thought. *How profound is that? The scars we endure in life really do affect our ability to "feel."*

"Some say scar tissue is extremely tough," said Ellyn, "and
some say an old wound is easily torn if it hasn't healed properly."

"The body is amazing, really, ain't it?" said Paulina Wise
Woman. "The way it fixes shit and keeps on going."

For the purposes of this book, we have focused our attention
on how young people are pulled or pushed into the sex trade
by extenuating circumstances in their formative years, including childhood sexual abuse, rape, and lack of caregivers, and
into further exploitation, for commercial purposes or not. We
have also explored the resultant traumas and lack of perceived
choices that often result from this lifestyle. Many survivor-
led organizations around the world focus on healing this kind
of trauma without prescribing lifestyle choices for the people
who seek services. Many people who currently work or have
worked in the sex industry believe that it has empowered them
or otherwise impacted their lives in a positive way. Many others believe that their involvement in the sex industry has been
destructive to the core of their being.

We make no judgment on staying or leaving the industry of
sex, but regardless of where someone falls on the continuum,
sexual trauma is often the root cause of that person's involvement, and so services need to be available to heal these old
traumas, no matter the person's choice to remain in the industry or to leave. In later chapters, we will discuss alternative

healing strategies and creating safety as means of overcoming and dealing with old sexual trauma.

Additionally, although we do not focus specifically on buyers, facilitators, pimps, perpetrators of violence, or abusive partners in this book, we have to mention that all participants involved are part of the same cycle of trauma, and, generally speaking, those who exploit others have been exploited themselves. This is essentially how it works—one ends up as exploiter or exploited in this cycle, but it is all a result of the same root cause. If we do not see the root and pluck it out, we will never make a significant difference in addressing any of these issues.

One advocate who identifies as a "survivor" of the sex industry shares the following story of meeting a young woman at an art exhibit, and the ways in which the ensuing discussion encouraged her to examine her current views on the subject.

She was a young woman, about twenty-two or twenty-three, pretty, and dressed in a very short skirt.

"So, were you at that conference on human trafficking?" she asked me.

"Yeah," I answered. "I spoke at the beginning. Were you there?"

She looked up at me, slowly raising her eyes to meet mine, and a slight smile crept across her face. "Yeah, I was there, too, sort of. . . . Well, I was outside protesting. You know, protesting the conference."

"Oh, that's right; I remember there were people protesting."

I know I looked puzzled. Here was a young, attractive woman, barely out of her teens, and she was taking a stand against protecting exploited people.

I suspected it was more complicated than that, and I wanted to understand, but before I could even ask, she offered, "I was protesting because of law enforcement involvement and all the laws they're trying to pass to make it more difficult for sex workers." She glanced at me again with a look that was at first assertive but quickly became anticipatory. I felt momentarily conflicted, my eyes questioning hers, I'm sure, and then I looked away to avoid the slight discomfort of the moment.

She was a stranger to me, someone I had just met in an art gallery, and it was only a chance social encounter. I didn't know what to say. On the one hand, I respected her thinking on this subject: if people want to sell their bodies, then they should have the right. Antiquated views of sexuality have been part of the problem. All of the repression around bodily desires over hundreds of years has caused a backlash of hidden perversities. Is it not better to bring openness to the issue and allow people to do as they will with their bodies? I might have said these same words to someone like me years ago.

Instead, I had no answer. I replied, "I've been working to stop violence against women for over a decade now—especially around sexual abuse and assault. It's difficult to talk about the sex industry—there are so many layers, and a lot of people have been deeply hurt."

An older man chimed in, "Good for you. Thanks for all your work." *Let's put a period on this conversation and move you out of here*, he seemed to say without words.

The young woman was silent and looked down. She did not say anything more. The moment was over, but I had a glimpse into a forgotten feeling, a long-ago scar. Is it really possible to separate the soul from the needs of the flesh? Is it possible not to feel deeply and to compartmentalize life into packages that don't touch one another? I know the answers to these questions, and of course they are yes and yes. I have done it.

I left the art gallery and continued walking through the San Francisco night, wondering about the girl and the conversation and what she might really have been thinking. I was wondering about her life and her past, her family and upbringing, and how those things had influenced her perception. I couldn't judge any of it, and wouldn't. I felt in a way as if I were like her, and even today, I could sense a confusion and ambiguity within myself. Scars of an earlier time that had left only a mark, no longer the pain of the original wound—I could see them, touch them, but I had trouble accessing the feeling. I had taken trauma and swallowed it into me as a girl, so that when I began to dance in bars and for bachelor parties, it was no big deal. Sex with strangers was no big deal, either, but even then some little place inside me screamed out.

For me, there were motives. I wanted to be seen, and I wanted to be known. I loved the taste of momentary power and the illusion that it could stay. I had always loved the illusion, whether it was the illusion of sexual power or the illusion of being loved in the moment. Sometimes I gambled recklessly. For me, the compartments were at war, and I eventually wanted a truce. That truce did not come for years, though, and many battles took place before a peace treaty was signed.

⟡

Sexual trauma is a scar. Whether it occurs in childhood, adolescence, or adulthood, it leaves a mark that cannot be erased.
We have had long talks about this subject—discussions that
have led to discourse on whether prostitution, forced or chosen, leaves the same trauma. We've lamented our own so-called
"chosen" paths and the lingering soul sickness of separating
body from spirit. We've struggled with old, old pain that affects
our ability to be intimate with another, to love, to accept love,
to trust another human being whom we care about. We know
that this pain, these old scars, are remnants of an earlier time—
a time when we had no choice but to give body to the one who
asked for it, and a time when we freely gave body to anyone
who asked (and we told ourselves that we were choosing to do
so), because it no longer mattered and we were separated from
the connection. Sometimes the giving of the body made us feel
special, unique, and powerful, and sometimes it made us feel
loved and desired; sometimes it failed miserably and left only
emptiness. At some point, we were able to separate successfully, shrug our shoulders at sex partners, roll our eyes, and
walk away, but this, too, had its long-term consequences.

Survivors of sexual trauma, like survivors of war, have
deep trauma, but because sexual trauma is often minimized in
our culture, and because it has happened to so many people and
in such varying manners and circumstances, its exact impact is
difficult to research and detect. Dr. K. Elan Jung, in his book,
Sexual Trauma: A Challenge, Not Insanity, lists a number of
documented and startling statistics: 20 to 25 percent of all chil-

dren are sexually abused; one female in four and one male in eight are sexually abused as children.[64] He also states, based on his thirty years of working with victims of sexual abuse, "Each and every victim came to me with agonizing self-doubts, paralyzing mistrust, inability to be intimate, self-loathing, self-destruction, confusion, and anger. They suffered a plethora of psychiatric disorders covering the spectrum, ranging from the most severe and disabling anxiety and panic attacks, depression, dissociation, delusion, hallucination, and other psychiatric disorders." Further, he concludes, "There is no other event that makes the human mind as confused, painful, and destructive as sexual abuse and traumatic sexual experiences."[65]

The whispered anecdotes of despair and trauma that so many endure are common to survivors of childhood sexual abuse. Not all early sexual trauma leads to prostitution, exploitation, and/or a history of negative sexual experiences; however, it does have an impact on the victim's life in a multitude of seen and unseen ways. Many argue that not all prostitution is precipitated by early sexual trauma, but this research is inconclusive and difficult to capture. Trauma, in any case, is a challenging demon to wrestle.

These are our precious scars, seen and unseen. We touch them with care and reverence. They've created new skin on our body and souls. They've become part of who we are now. We are different than who we were before, and scars remind us of this simple fact. A physical scar changes the skin forever. An emotional scar changes the psyche forever, too. Scars don't go away; they change over time, perhaps diminishing, becoming

64. K. Elan Jung, *Sexual Trauma: A Challenge Not Insanity* (New York: Hudson Press, 2010), 32.
65. Ibid., 22.

less noticeable, but they are still there. The next three stories tell of the triumph and victory that we learn from our scars.

I have a scar on my left shoulder, a discoloration of skin making a disc of silver white, kind of shiny, round like a full moon, just like the moon was on the day my injury occurred in Kerala, India, as I played in the Arabian Sea. Pummeled by a wave and thrown to the ground underwater, I hit my head and shoulder on a rock and was nearly knocked out. I was bleeding when I surfaced, shaken, confused. A memory reminder of mortality, of the passing of youth, of the strength of the sea and its unforgiving playfulness toward those in human form—all of these thoughts surfaced in my awareness.

I will remember this scar and its teaching. Its significance in midlife is the knowledge that I can travel, swim, play, and dance under a round, white-silver moon that lights up the night, drink warm chai with milk at 5:00 a.m., and watch that moon over the ocean begin to fade as the day approaches. I also know that, for all the magic of life, there are things that hurt us and throw us to the ground at times. How we get up, how we choose to live, and to whom and what we give our attention are opportunities where our scars can be our guides and instructors. Nothing is to be taken for granted—not safety, not love, not kindness, not the passing of the years, not the earth or the sea.

When I touch the disc of a scar on my shoulder, I know that I am part of the moon, the sea, and time. My blood has mingled with the salt, sand, and sky, and we are one. My full-moon scar is the stigmata of this knowledge.

I stood at the edge of the water hesitantly, a blanket wrapped tightly round about me, not really for warmth, but more for protection. I watched as women, and some men, ventured into the waters, shedding their towels and lowering their naked bodies into the healing waters. Bare skin of different hues covered the landscape wherever I turned. Most had scars, some small and barely noticeable, others more pronounced, covering faces and buttocks, some maybe even considered repulsive.

A tall black woman walked elegantly to the edge of a pool. Her head was held high, her chin up. Her hair, braided, was curled into a bun and secured with vibrant red and gold yarn. She avoided my eyes, however, as she dropped her colorful towel and stepped confidently down the old brick steps. Jagged scars ran down her back; marks from generations of abuse, slavery, violent whippings. She smiled softly to herself as the warm water engulfed her body. Closing her eyes, she slowly immersed herself and disappeared under the waters. I watched her swim, gracefully, underwater.

The sun was warm on my skin as I bent down and put the tips of my fingers into the baths; a delicious heat traveled through my body. A cluster of people caught my eye, and I turned to follow their sounds—of laughter or crying, I couldn't quite be sure.

As I turned, a brown-skinned woman of sixty or seventy

smiled at me. She had been watching me, I thought. I smiled back. She looked in the direction of the others and said sweetly, "Some paddle in the shallow waters."

I turned and followed her eyes to a sandy embankment. Indeed, many were walking, or kicking their feet, at the edge of a clear blue ocean. Most were naked and unashamed, although some, like me, carried towels or blankets either in their hands or around their bodies.

The woman turned again. Her hair, long and gray, maybe almost white, was tied in a simple ponytail that ran down her back. "Over here," she said, "there are ice-cold pools. The water travels from the highest snowcapped mountains." I nodded, listening intently. "The ice may take your breath away"—she laughed—"but it will also take away your worries." She pointed in another direction. "And here . . . ," she said. "Here are the hot pools. The water springs up from the ground, water thousands of years old that covered the earth before mankind began. The water may burn your flesh, but it may burn your fears as well."

I smiled, curious anxiety covering my face. "Why on earth would anyone do that?" I exclaimed.

"Ahh, my sweet child," she murmured. "To be made whole, one must endure fire and one must endure ice." Her words, laced with wisdom, dripped out of her mouth like sweet honey. "If you first go into the icy waters, then quickly go into the fire pool, you will not be frozen and you will not be burned." She held out her arm, her tanned skin smooth, without blemish or spot. I reached out and touched her arm softly. Her skin was soft and supple, not revealing her age at all. I smiled again.

"You go into the waters often?" I asked.

"Yes, my dear, I come as often as I can. When the dirt of life tarnishes my skin, I come and bathe here. I am no longer afraid." She bowed ever so slightly—a sign of love and respect. I bowed back. She turned and walked in the direction of the others. As she walked, I noticed a slight limp, and deep lacerations down her side and her legs. She, too, had scars. Fascinated by her wisdom and her patience for teaching, I wanted to follow her.

Sensing my longing, she turned back. "You may paddle in the shallow waters," she said, pointing. "You may kick your feet gently through the sand. You may bathe in the pools of fire and ice, frozen doubts and healing warmth." She looked out, past the others, to the deep parts of the sea. "Other times it may be necessary to swim out farther, to the deeper waters where the mermaids swim. You might find yourself in a whirlpool at times, being sucked down into too-familiar waters. Don't be afraid—you will not drown. You have learned over the years to survive in air and water. You can swim through the deep like a fish, or like a bird soar high above the clouds. You can adapt. You can endure."

My eyes filled with tears. Hopeful, I turned to the first pool. It was fuller now. A couple huddled in the corner in each other's arms, allowing the waters to slowly cover their bodies. A large, pale woman helped her sister down the steps. Both had deep red scars; they slowly entered the waters together. The younger sister leaned back in the waters and began to float, allowing the soft ripples to slowly rock her to and fro. A younger woman sat at the edge, curled in a blanket, looking at the waters with longing, not quite ready to enter the healing.

Then I heard the voice of wisdom again, a slight whisper. I searched the horizon for her scarred form, but she had disappeared. "To enter into solidarity with one who is suffering doesn't mean we have to talk with them about our own suffering," she said sweetly. I closed my eyes so I could hear her clearly. "Speaking about our own suffering is seldom helpful for one who is in pain. A wounded healer is one who can listen to a person in pain without having to speak about his or her own wounds."

I nodded to the invisible speaker.

"When we have gone through a great struggle, a time of pain, an intense scarring, we can listen with great compassion and love without having to mention our own experiences. We have to trust that our own bandaged wounds will allow us to listen to others with our own whole being."

Yes, I said without speaking.

"That, my dear, is healing."[66]

I dropped my blanket and turned to the young woman, extending my hand. Her eyes looked up at my face and traveled down my body. My scars were now open to her view; the marks left by abusive partners, family members, even society, seemed to glow in the sunlight. I was not ashamed. I was proud now, proud that I had endured, excited about the healing I had begun. "It's okay," I said, almost silently. "We can go together."

She smiled and stood. "We can go together," she repeated, and stepped confidently into the blue wetness. I lowered myself in; the softness of the waters ran over my body. I, too, closed my eyes, like the women before me, and allowed the waters to cover my face and then my hair.

---

66. Adapted from Henri J. M. Nouwen, *The Wounded Healer: Ministry in Contemporary Society* (New York: Doubleday, 1972).

I would take many trips to the waters, some for refreshment, many out of necessity, but every time I entered consciously into healing, the scars on my body faded slightly. Other people, unless I trusted them enough to really open up, wouldn't even have noticed their existence. Sure, if I ran my fingers over my chest, I could still feel the ridges in my skin, and I was glad. It was a reminder of all I had conquered.

My lover has scars on his back. One scar is about six inches long and a quarter of an inch wide, like a line that runs across his lower back, and above it is a tiny circle scar, perhaps from the same accident. On his left shoulder is a scar in the shape of a cloud or a cluster—a scar that I find deep and thick and palpable to the touch without looking at it.

I touch his scars with the tenderness of a mother to a baby. Lightly at first, and then with a soft intensity, I massage and move the skin. They are scars of time, injury, pain. Some are long forgotten, and some hold memories of the trauma that the body felt: a deep cut, an accident, a fight. His memories, unknown to me, make up the change of skin and the layer upon layer of tissue that grew to protect the wound. Every wound ends in a scar.

I ask him the story of each scar that I have grown to know. He tells me, and sometimes I forget the details; sometimes he tells me more. I touch the scars and feel the energy of years, time, memory, and form all bound together by fibrous compositions of proteins that have grown distinctly different from the surrounding and original skin.

Touching a scar is distinctly intimate. Once a place of trauma and pain, it is now a hidden site that most will never know. To know a scar is to care deeply for another. If I know his scars, then I know that I love, for scars tell me the stories that I do not hear, the stories that I am not a part of. If he takes the time to know and touch my scars, then he will get to know some part of me that is unexpressed, tender, waiting. It will mean that he cares enough to come into contact with all that makes up a body, both lovely and not lovely, and not to be afraid or opposed to seeing my humanness fully. This is a gift more precious than rare jewels and more desired than all other gifts. To love with intensity, to touch with true intimacy, and to honor past pain is to be fully human and alive.

My scars make up a part of me. They've changed my body in some way, but they don't define me. They are a part of the story line of my life. When I was three, I fell off my tricycle careening around a corner of the driveway, and there is a linear scar on the back of my left hand and a small scar under my bottom lip. When I was fourteen, I jumped out of a car and busted my face on the pavement of a road; I have a scar under my chin to remind me that I could've been killed if my head had landed differently. When I was seventeen, I had a surgery that left a large, raised keloid scar of several inches along my right groin. This scar is only ever seen by those who have seen me naked and is very apparent, and yet the majority of men who have touched me over the years have never mentioned it. And there are others, too, perhaps smaller and with less memorable stories, yet all are a piece of fabric covering I wear called skin.

I have learned to honor the scar tissue of my body and the places unseen to any eye. I honor my own past pain as I do the pain of the beloved man who lies beside me some nights. I feel his rich brown skin infused with shrapnel of another time and the mystery of things I will never know. Our scars, a part of the story but not the entirety of it, the ones seen and unseen, remain our way of connecting to what is more than human in those whom we have grown to love.

PART III

THE WAY HOME

TO OURSELVES

CHAPTER 11

DIVING INTO THE DEPTHS

Take me . . . Yes, take me . . . But you know best
Where the sea calmly opens its blue road.
I'm wearier than your oldest tower;
Somewhere I've left my heart aside.[67]

As we have indicated extensively in previous chapters, sexual trauma and exploitation at an early age have numerous effects and consequences for women. The stories we have told are real, as are the conflicts within and without when we discuss these challenging issues. However, each woman affected by early abuse has a unique journey. Each person experiences the pain and trauma in her own way and deals with it as best she can at the time. There is no set response to sexual trauma; however, one of the commonalities is the loss or minimization of one's self-worth. Some may act out sexually, some may shut down, some might hide or build walls, and some may relinquish all boundaries and head down a path of destruction. The effects

---

67 Adrienne Rich, "White Night," in *The Fact of a Doorframe* (New York: W. W. Norton & Co., 1984), 197.

are profound and painful, and they steal life away. Because the wounds are so very deep, the solutions and the healing also have to emerge from a very deep place within the soul of a person. In this last section of the book, our focus is on healing ourselves and the world around us—a spiral journey that requires us to look deeply inward and bring the treasures that we discover to an outward place that in turn helps to heal our world.

The world we live in is a broken one where humans have the capacity to do great harm to one another, as we have done to the planet. We also have the capacity to do great good. But this is not the easiest or most readily known way for most of our world systems or for our individual lives. The patriarchal worldview is the very air that we breathe without question or awareness; it infiltrates our religions, our families, and our societal structures and institutions.

In order for women to heal from the damage caused by these systems—by the consequences of exploitation, shame, and abuse, and by the subsequent minimization of these experiences—we must foster awareness. This opportunity to become aware begins with looking at the effects on the self, at the internalized messages that cause us to split the true self away from the expectations of the patriarchal family at an early age and then to live from that place of falseness that separates us from others and our own feelings.

Rita Nakashima Brock, a feminist Christian theologian, states in her book *Journeys by Heart: A Christology of Erotic Power* that "if we are to understand fully what it means to be human, we must see what the oppression of women costs our families and society. . . . We internalize most deeply and powerfully our earliest relationships, from which come our ability or inability to internalize later loves and losses, to coexist humanely with others, and to continue to flourish and grow as persons."[68]

Diving into the deep waters of our individual lives is the beginning. In that underwater journey, we begin to explore the places of wreckage and the treasures hidden inside. It is a journey to self and requires more fortitude and courage than many can muster at times. When we examine our own brokenness and our participation in the brokenness of others, we are then able to look at the patriarchal structures of our society with different eyes. We can see more clearly how we use and abuse power, and how others use and abuse power against us; we can see more clearly the privileges and biases we carry. We are more able to acknowledge the privilege of white experience, of a "good education," of being American or European, and of socioeconomic status. We can also see how oppressions of race and gender are at the core of much of our suffering, and certainly at the core of most all sexual trauma and suffering. Feminists have sought over the last several decades to address this suffering and to transform it, so that women may better love themselves. Unfortunately, these efforts, too, have been co-opted by our paternalistic society. In our broken-heartedness, we often suffer alone, continuing to look for answers outside ourselves and within the framework of a male-dominated system that holds no honest solutions to our pain.

This is why we must dive into the deep waters of our lives, which hold old and buried traumas and messages that tell us

68. Rita Nakashima Brock, *Journeys by Heart: A Christology of Erotic Power* (New York: Crossroad Publishing Company, 1988), 4.

who we should be (and the consequences of refusing these roles), and into the places where oppression has defined us. As we embark upon this journey to ourselves, we can begin to shift the patriarchal structure of this world and the damage it has caused, one decision at a time, as one new awareness opens the door for another.

We must also be willing to break the silence of our own pain. In poetry or prose, song or dance, with individuals, in small groups or auditoriums, we must be willing to confront the societal constructs that steal our voice and blind our eyes. All of us would be best served if women of every worldview, along with their male allies, came together and ignited a global dialogue that looked honestly at these intersections of pain and violence that have affected us for far too long. Silence, as we have learned in previous chapters, is a breeding ground for abuse to continue. We must use our voice, and it indeed needs to be a collective one.

Imagine that as women we were brought up and taught from an early age to love and trust ourselves. Our individual lives would look so very different, as would our collective lives. Imagine what it would be like if we as females were seen as treasures from the cradle to the grave, if all phases of our lives—maiden, mother, and crone years—were celebrated like the phases of the moon. If we were thought to be beautiful throughout all of our changes, if we were nurtured and loved all the years of our lives, then our hearts would be expansive and we would be leading, loving, and nurturing this world to a new place.

This next story is about a woman who began to notice the effects of linear time (as we all do), but who understood that things are not always as they appear and so passed this wisdom down through generations, so that they, too, could learn to trust themselves.

Her hands today were much older than she remembered. The veins were more apparent than before, against the added folds and crinkled-paper quality of skin worn by sun and years. They had become lived-in hands—hands that had changed diapers, cleaned floors, typed papers, written letters on real stationery, fixed broken things, held other hands, and touched another with love. They looked years older than the rest of her, but she was not ashamed. These hands showed the signs of living the more difficult path, of not choosing the easy way. These hands knew the depths of pain, and they also knew the amazing buoyancy of joy. They had reached above, held on, searched below, and felt—really felt—what it was like to be alive and living.

One of these hands took the hand of the little girl and held it gently, lovingly, but firmly in her own. The little girl's trusting and hopeful hand was unknowing of any suffering in life, unaware of the mysteries, but somewhere in her cells knew the dance, trusted the movement, and held tightly to the hand that knew more of this life. And so together they walked and watched a little of night at the edges of a cornfield under a most starry and brightly lit sky.

There was a comfort between them. The little girl said to the woman, "Grandmother, please tell me about the moon—it never looks the same from night to night. What is the moon?"

The older woman looked down at the girl and then pointed her finger to the orb in the sky. "That is the moon," she said. "The moon has its own stories to tell. It looks different to us depending on where the earth and the sun are positioned and where we are standing, but it is always the same. If you observe closely, you will see this for yourself."

Years later, when the little girl had grown and her own hands were becoming worn with time, work, and caring for others, she would look to the moon and remember her grandmother. She would also remember her own stories—stories she and the moon shared. Secrets the moon had kept for her over the years, tales of love and loss the moonlight had held as her confidante. The moon had remained the same—a constant witness to life, a silent and uncompromising observer, a friend with stories of its own. What is the moon? It is what you see and experience. One can only point it out to another; we must each learn its mysteries for ourselves.

There is a ladder.
The ladder is always there. . . .
We know what it is for. . . .[69]

We know the ladder downward, but we don't know the precise way to the depths of the wreckage within. We are amazed by the

---

69. Adrienne Rich, "Diving into the Wreck," in *The Fact of a Doorframe* (New York: W. W. Norton & Co., 1984), 162.

unusual quality of the creatures we have never before encountered, and we are more skilled at seeing the ones who are poison-
ous or dangerous to us. We help one another by pointing the way
and telling our stories of triumph and failure from the journey.

When we truly begin to look, we see both the terror and the
joy, and we see the terror that must be passed through to get to
the joy. We see the facing of the self that must be experienced
prior to release from any bondage. We see that the fiercest captor, the true slaveholder, the dominatrix of the soul, eventually
lies, breeds, and lives within us and must be challenged if we
are really to live our lives and to assume the destiny to which
we are born. The abuse inflicted by others becomes our own
mantra in time, and we become the unwilling captors and participants in our own cycle of pain, torture, and abuse. We learn
to inflict upon the precious self what we have learned from earlier times and from the unkindness of those who were, perhaps,
also hanging from chains forged by the unkindness of others.

But all chains can be broken.

We let go of the ladder and we fall through water like the
air swirling about us, bubbles of breath and fear, despair, longing. Do we survive? It is a trap, a long way down, no known return, no way out. How do we survive this fall and this choice?
How do we emerge once again to breathe the air of the humans? How do we live on?

First, we practice. We loosen our grip on the rope, one
finger at a time. Maybe we take one hand off the wood or the
rope of the ladder. Then, in minutes that seem like hours, we
practice the act of letting go. Fingers that held tightly to the ladder simply release and drop downward toward the wreck that

we must explore, the treasure we must find. Although we know that treasure lies below, we are terrified of the drop downward and the possibilities of failure—or success. But drop we must, falling into the abyss of the unknown; the journey will show us the way, and we will be caught by our own arms in time.

This we are learning. This is learning not easily retained, not readily remembered.

Each descent and exploration is its own unique journey. We may drop many times before we find the treasure that is ours alone. We may miss the treasure altogether at times but find other beautiful and useful things. Sometimes, as in the next story, our descent takes us to the land of dreams, where we explore other worlds not so very far away.

There were mysteries that continually called to her and beckoned her under. Never in the daylight did they call; it was always after darkness fell and usually just before sleep. Interesting murmurs of sea sounds and creatures from underneath, not birds above, beckoned with the swaying movement of unhurried consistency. *Not going anywhere; nowhere to go but here and see what is here, face and acknowledge what is here, hear the sea and know what is true.*

Many times she just ignored the call and went about her business of importance and living in time, doing her work, not paying attention to dreams or desires but remaining in her practical mind.

Staying busy had been a coping strategy that had saved

her from herself for many years. In her early twenties, she had become extremely depressed and anxious, full of dread and trying to fit into a life that was not her own. A therapist told her to "stay busy," so she did. Busy saved her, but it also kept her from seeing underneath. It kept her from acknowledging what was really wrong and what would eventually shackle her with chains of her own making. There was joy in those years as well, but she did not fully feel it because her mind kept both the joy and the pain at bay, and not too close so that they might touch. But this strategy no longer worked for her, because the nagging inevitability of opening the closed doors of her heart and facing those things she hid from herself became ever-present in her consciousness. As with a dress that no longer fit well or a costume falling apart, she had to change into something that worked better for her. She had to change in order to "feel."

So when they came calling one night, she listened and followed and did not run away. Strange-voiced folk from another place underneath with something to say waited patiently, with compassion in their unusual eyes. There were three of them, with wavy, shiny, salty, weed-filled hair pulled back tightly from their faces. Faces beyond human form, beautiful, but not as we think on the surface—their beauty was beyond our usual mind.

The woman felt out of her league and did not know how to respond or what to say, and yet somehow she also knew the place and the faces and she sensed envy rising within her.

They knew this immediately and reached out to her. "Don't expect so much of yourself," spoke one. "You mustn't be so angry with yourself. You must be kind and patient to yourself. You are still in human form." She continued, "Keep doing this work. I have been in this form for a very long time, and I'm going back to the fold. You will be in this form, too, one day, but now, be patient with your humanness."

And with those words, she was silent and swimming away with the other merfolk creatures, gentle as gossamer silk on a breeze, gentle as a fish's tail through water. The woman wanted to ask questions but waited in the depths instead. She was unafraid to stay but needed to surface. There would be more trips and more messages to find, more ground to explore, and she would find a way in the world of time to learn these lessons from underneath, and to bring them with grace into her being.

Sexual exploitation and abuses will not ever be adequately addressed until as a society, or as citizens of the world, we begin to understand how we use sex as a weapon and a tool of power. The roots of using another person for personal satisfaction, gain, or profit, or as instrument—especially in the use and abuse of women—are embedded deep within a culture that worships the acquisition of power at all costs. Although we have made great social strides in understanding and unraveling racism, it remains. The same is true for homophobia and gender discrimination; we have made headway toward treating all people with respect, but the patriarchal culture that is dominant in most of the world still prevails unconsciously.

For women, society defines our worth, value, and lovability, even our beauty, and we believe these definitions, for the most part. Sexual exploitation, as with abuse, is a result of the misuse of power, just as domestic violence and sexual assault are abuses of power—ultimately not about sex or the erotic, but about treating another human as an object to be used and consumed and not as a person of value and worth. This is the commonality between gender oppression, sexual violence, racism, and other evils that negate the worth of our fellow and sister human beings.

Ultimately, individuals must define for themselves what constitutes abuse and how they choose to live. Becoming aware of the places of wreckage in our lives, and making choices about what we need to do to heal, address, or ignore these places, is up to each person to embrace.

In our girls' group one evening, we sat around in a circle, as we usually did—able to see each other and to practice active listening and being present. If nothing else, at least we didn't have anyone behind us and we could keep our eyes on each other. We were still mistrustful, still cautious, but it worked.

In the middle of the circle, in a plastic box on the floor, were pencils, pens, and crayons. Sometimes we added stickers and glitter and other decorative materials. As we talked, we doodled mindlessly in our composition notebooks or journals. We also made time, however, to create. We had been learning as a group to express ourselves in words, in pictures, sometimes in dance, sometimes in theater. We found that these creative expressions of our lives, our joys, and our pains afforded us a glimpse into one another's pasts and futures in ways verbal dialogue could not. We had been working on our own road maps, documenting things that had come up for us week by week, as we dove together. We had all become artists, writing the stories of our lives, both those things we had experienced and that which was to come. We practiced writing the music to which we would all dance, the themes to our own songs. Individually, and yet together, we redesigned and reinvented our future, no longer willing to float aimlessly through our destiny, but motivated to swim deep, to press and push past our fears and anxieties.

Karla stood up and cleared her throat. She had experienced more pain in her short life than many faced in a lifetime.

"I'ma read a poem by Audre Lorde," she said, smiling. "Grandma printed it out for me." She kissed her lips and pumped her chest. "Love you, Grandma."

The girls laughed.

Grandma was a volunteer who spent her evenings pouring wisdom into young people, sharing her story and baring the scars on her soul. She had printed the poem, and Karla had painstakingly decorated it, adorned it with images of girls and women and mermaids.

Karla began:

"For those of us who live at the shoreline . . ."

She read slowly and deliberately. The girls listened. Nodded. Understood. They had experienced living at the shoreline, watching the waves lap at their feet, too unsure to step into the surf. They nodded knowingly, remembering the doorways, the openings, the opportunities for choice, yet too often not choosing.

Karla continued on and then concluded:

"So it is better to speak / Remembering . . . we were never meant to survive."[70]

The girls continued to nod. They knew these words. They were all learning how to speak, and they were all scared.

There were many weeks like this, though—weeks when we pushed past the fear and just spoke. Sometimes we read poetry, sometimes we wrote our own. Sometimes we cried, sometimes we laughed, but always we cheered each other on. Even the quieter girls slipped us folded-up papers with stories and artwork that gave us glimpses into the recesses of their souls. We developed community. We wrote our own trauma narratives and continued the practice of using our voices. At first it was difficult to write without judgment—even stories we knew intimately became more critical under the watchful eyes of others—but most often the judgment was our own. We fostered discussions of difficult topics and swam together in treacherous waters. We knew we were taking powerful first steps, whether we shared our stories or not, by putting on paper the remnants of experience that we had been dragging around in oversize luggage for years. We were making beautiful what had been torturous; we were sharing parts of ourselves with those we didn't yet know while honoring those whose stories we knew too well. We battled the fear that lay waiting in the silence. We faced it head-on because we knew there was no other way.

---

70. Audre Lorde, "A Litany for Survival," in The Black Unicorn: Poems (New York: W. W. Norton & Co., 1995).

The concept of diving requires us to be willing to face ourselves with the same scrutiny that we apply to others, and we need the mirror of others whom we trust to indicate whether or not we are being honest with ourselves.

The two of us have both experienced lying on the bottom of the ocean, feeling defeated, lost, unloved, and, most of all, bereft of hope that we mattered enough or would ever matter enough to anyone. We still struggle with all of these issues, but together we have gained an awareness of the depths of these soul-wrenching doubts and combined our toolboxes to find a way to explore, confront, acknowledge, accept, and rise again. We have learned much as individuals over the years, and we have survived—and, together, we have a found a way to gain hope and experience joy more fully. Ultimately, going deep requires that we also find the way upward with more strength, courage, and wherewithal for the journey.

In the chapters that follow, we will discuss some of the resources that we have discovered. We will explore learning to live in our skin, loving deeply, embodying and celebrating our sexuality without harm to our souls, finding power in the erotic, being present to ourselves and others, the power of empathy, and the transformation that gratitude brings. Simply put, there are no easy answers and no shortcuts to healing from early sexual trauma and abuse, or from childhood neglect or abandonment. Unfortunately, those traumas leave an imprint on our souls that we must learn to live with, and then live beyond, if we are to be truly whole and alive. It is a process that we grapple with daily; some days we are on top of the world, and others we are at the bottom of the sea.

We all find our ways to live in this world. Some of us choose to shut out the soul's needs and longings, and to live in a more cynical or judgmental mind that minimizes all it doesn't want to understand. Some live all their lives shut off from deeper yearnings and knowledge. Others minimize, ignore, and hide through sex, drugs, self-medication of all kinds, recreation, anger, or just keeping busy—and all this is okay, too, if that is what they choose and they are hurting no one else in the process. The challenge is for the ones who cannot ignore the deeper call and the ones who are unafraid to explore what has wounded them and how they can begin to heal. This is the "road less traveled" that Dr. Scott Peck talked about twenty-plus years ago, and it is the heart of psychological inquiry.[71] This is the wisdom way of feminist/womanist consciousness. This is also the mystical path of most faith traditions. It is not the easy way. But it may be the best way to get home.

---

71. Morgan Scott Peck. *The Road Less Traveled: A New Psychology of Love, Traditional Values and Spiritual Growth.* (Simon & Schuster).

CHAPTER 12

SEEING THE REFLECTION IN THE WATER

Whoever fights monsters should see to it that in the process he does not become a monster.[72]

The Greek myth of Narcissus, the beautiful boy who spurned the love of the nymphs and fell in love with his own reflection in the water, has been retold many times and in many ways. It is a story of warning that informs the audience of the danger of seeing only the superficial self, of falling in love with outer beauty only, and of expecting perfection. In almost all of the stories, Narcissus dies because he cannot bear to leave his reflection or even drink of the water beneath him, lest he alter his reflection. He dies without a connection to anything, not even himself.

This myth also inspired the name of a personality disorder in the fourth and fifth editions of the *Diagnostic and Statistical*

---

72. Frederich Nietzsche quote, accessed by: https://www.goodreads.com/quotes/18463-whoever-fights-monsters-should-see-to-it-that-in-the

Manual of Mental Disorders.[73] Narcissistic personality disorder is characterized by impairments in personality and interpersonal functioning, including lack of empathy, preoccupation with self-identity, exaggerated self-appraisal, and the inability to establish real intimacy.[74]

The late Swiss psychologist Alice Miller wrote *The Drama of the Gifted Child*, which was translated into English in 1981. In this work, she was one of the first to discuss the healthy narcissistic development of children, which occurs when the baby or child finds him or herself mirrored in the mother and the mother is attentive to providing the "emotional climate and understanding for the child's needs."[75] Generally speaking, and as a rather simple but not complete summary, injury to a child's early, basic narcissistic needs sets the stage for psychological challenges of some type later in life. Additionally, and as we pointed out in earlier chapters, if secure attachments are not formed early in life with caregivers who assist the child's emotional development, then injuries to a child's sense of self are likely to occur. And since most of the population has not been parented perfectly and, to a greater or lesser degree, all people suffer from some form of early narcissistic injury, we are all in some ways struggling with issues of healthy self-esteem, self-image challenges, and the ways in which we hold and use power. All of us at some point in our lives find ourselves staring into the pool of water, unable to see what is around us and focused completely on our own faces, on our own needs and wants, and perhaps stuck in our own pain. We may stay there,

---

73. American Psychiatric Association, "Narcissistic Personality Disorder," in *Diagnostic and Statistic Manual of Mental Disorders* V (Arlington, VA: American Psychiatric Publishing, 2013).
74. Ibid.
75. Alice Miller, *The Drama of the Gifted Child* (New York: Basic Books, 1981), 32.

unconscious and unaware, for a while, but with a little luck we will see the trees and the birds reflected in the sky above and notice the ripples of the water that reflect our image. It's all a matter of where we put our focus. If we expand our focus, we notice that there is much more going on than what we perceive based on our emotions or our current state of mind.

In the myth of Narcissus, his focus is entirely on himself and his beauty, and his world is consequently limited. He has no vision of other possibilities. Sometimes when we stare into the eyes of another human being, we see only our own reflection, and our thoughts and judgments stare back at us. If we are fortunate enough to notice that what we see is not the whole picture but our own illusions, based on our own thoughts and feelings, then we can begin to notice and actually glimpse a bigger reality where we are not the sole reflection but where there are millions of reflections—the sky, the birds, the trees—and we are merely a part of many.

Healing ourselves and our world requires us to have the courage to see more, to broaden our vision, to see past our reflected image and to understand that what we think, feel, and know is important but limited. All of our feelings and thoughts are based on our perceptions of reality. It is only in reaching beyond what we think we know that we are able to really see much more.

◦❧◦

"Mirror, mirror, on the wall, who's the fairest of them all?"[76]

The scene of Narcissus staring into the pool and seeing nothing of beauty or value, symbolizes perhaps not seeing our true selves at all, but rather seeing only what we have been told that others want to see. Throughout this book, we have talked about being objectified by others—especially those who pretend to care for us—and how this objectification and emotional abuse play into the hands of sexual exploitation of all kinds. When someone sees another person or thing as an "it"—an object, a thing to be used by or useful only to others—then that person can justify whatever he or she wants to do with this "thing": discard it, trade it, save it for later, throw it away, destroy it—or, alternately, treasure it, put it on a shelf, own it, value it, sell it for more later on. All these options are available to us when we have a possession that is ours, and the same dynamic applies when we see a person as something we possess or "own."

This is the bottom line in relationships where domestic violence is present, and in the very roots of exploitation, racism, and violence against any human being. We buy, we sell, we own—we are human and they are not. On one level, it is very simple and easy to see, but in a deeper sense it is a slippery concept to hold, because on some level so much of our thinking is built on the evaluation of others, their judgments, and value through our monetary and other systems. We are conditioned from the time we are small children to evaluate other human beings, and ourselves, on societal scales that assign worth based on a variety of criteria. It seems a natural inclination of the mind to assign worth in neat packages that we hold throughout

---

76. The Brothers Grimm, "Snow White," *Grimms' Fairy Tales* (1812).

our lives and according to which we unconsciously live out our days. This is the strength of the ego, and it rules our planet. Societal constructs tell us it is better to be rich than poor, better to be male than female, lighter-skinned than darker-skinned, smart than dumb, educated than uneducated, pretty than ugly, and so on. With our packaged understanding of what is greater than and of more value than ourselves, we then equate power with those who hold the worth and exercise power over those who have less.

In simplistic terms, we do this throughout all of our relationships to a greater or lesser degree, often based on the role that we play and our belief in who is holding the power. But until we recognize what we have been trained to do, and that it is part of our societal makeup, we will not be able fully to understand, address, or effectively discuss issues such as domestic violence, child abuse, or the exploitation of people for sex or labor. All of these issues have the same root in power over another.

The confounding complications of this dynamic are especially noticeable when we try to understand issues such as forced prostitution versus prostitution as a chosen, "empowering" lifestyle—a discussion that comes up regularly for those of us who work to address the effects of the sex industry on people's lives. But if we understand the continuum of power and the assigning of value, it helps to unravel the question a bit more. Some come to the sex industry with more internal resources and societal privilege. Others come as children who have been seriously mistreated and have not received the love and security that they needed early in life. Many are somewhere in between. But all have survived in some way, regardless of whether they identify as sex worker, victim, or survivor, and it is not up to others to define their experience for them. Each person experiences holding—or losing—power in a manner unique to her and her situation.

A Victoria's Secret model posing provocatively holds societal power and value because of her beauty, celebrity status, money, and ability to create desire on various levels, whereas a young, lower-class woman posing for porn photos in a cheap hotel room holds much less value and certainly much less power. However, both are engaged in basically the same type of exchange, and both are using the commodity of their sexuality. Both are essentially in the same enterprise. But one has societal worth, and one does not; one holds the object status of treasure and envy, and the other is viewed as nothing but trash after use and consumption are completed. But even the Victoria's Secret model is expendable, because as she gets older, she will be replaced by a younger, newer model and her assigned worth will decline in that particular enterprise.

This is not just the case with sexual enterprises—it is also visible in numerous places where people are commodified and categorized by worth—but in this writing, we are focusing on the sexual perspective. A woman working as an escort can hold power-over through youth and beauty and their intoxicating, exhilarating effects, especially if she can sell her services for a lot of money. A woman supporting a drug habit through prostitution or being pimped out by a boyfriend who abuses her does not hold the same power-over—but both are part of the same continuum that objectifies sexuality and views it as a commodity to be bought and sold. Both have similar and different experiences within the same paradigm. Ultimately, like the latest model of automobile or technological device, both are expendable, replaceable, and eventually rendered obsolete. It's only a matter of time in a system that turns people into things and assigns them worth.

The challenge is to find the power of definition and worth within oneself, as the connection to the soul and the strength within is the only way out of this paradigm. There will always be those who seek to define your worth—whether it be a parent, a boyfriend, a coworker, or a system—and in the eyes of the world, they may succeed. But ultimately we are the definers of our lives, and we do not have to live under other people's labels, jealousies, insecurities, hostilities, or fears. It doesn't matter if you are called a supermodel or a whore—these labels are not your identity, and no one can make them so. You are so much more than any label, and your power comes from knowing that. You have the ability to define yourself, change yourself, and reinvent yourself at any time you choose. In doing so, we break societal chains.

Consequently, this bold act (every time it is chosen) builds the capacity for empathy and compassion for other beings, and thereby lessens our desire to judge, define, and evaluate others. Once our eyes are open to this knowledge, we will not be able to close them again.

The young black woman and the old yellow woman sat in the kitchen for hours, blending their lives so that what lay behind one and ahead of the other became indistinguishable.[77]

Although we are not young and black or old and yellow, such as in the story of *The Women of Brewster Place*, we developed our friendship through our collective work and the writing of this book. Using the concepts in this book, we have been able to recognize and articulate times when we have felt like outsiders, or times when we have lost our voice. Sometimes, merely the recognition alone has been enough to move us into a more healthy space. Other times we have needed, from each other and others, a little more direction and encouragement in order to continue along our healing journey. The following is a small example of how our experiences, although very different from one another, afforded us the opportunity to become reflections to each other in ways that both challenged and supported our respective growth. It is also an example of how the girls we worked with struggled in their own quests to establish restorative and reflective friendships in their own lives. Our hope is that, as women, we can all have a sojourner to walk this journey with us.

We sat in the corner of a crowded restaurant, sharing an appetizer and enjoying a glass of red wine, petite syrah. We were two very different women to the untrained eye, yet similarities even before birth had drawn us together. There was a spiritual connection, even though we differed in faith; there were also

---

77. Gloria Naylor, *The Women of Brewster Place*, (New York: Viking Penguin, Inc., 1982), 34.

emotional parallels, childhood similarities, rejections, aban-
donments. We were pulled together because of the work we
did, at least at first. We stayed together because of the work
we began to do. Inner work—the work of the heart and the
work of the spirit—became our real work. Though we had begun many years ago, alone, this kind of work can be truly ac-
complished only in the reflection of others. So we developed
a friendship—a friendship between two broken, untrusting
women; a friendship between two headstrong, heart-stronger
women—and it became a friendship of love.

Friendships, often minimized and trivialized in today's in-
dividualistic society, can be an amazingly simple yet indescrib-
ably complex way of seeing the reflection. As broken women,
we often struggle with friendships. Truly heartfelt, trusting,
transparent friendships are almost impossible for us. Many of
us grew up reciting such statements as:

"I don't get along with females."

"Most of my friends are boys."

"I get along better with men than with women."

We failed to recognize or acknowledge the reasons we were
drawn to men and, as we have described thus far, the reasons
men were drawn to us. We ran from the mirror of female friendships, and set artificial boundaries and unrealistic expectations
around our relationships with our same sex. Yet it is within
the confines of intimate friendships that we are free to examine
our lives in the reflection of others. Sure, we do examine and
reflect frequently throughout our days, yet oftentimes we do so
through comparison. We compare ourselves with other women,
using this comparison as a measure of our worth and value.

She's prettier, thinner, smarter, more eloquent.

She's cute, but I have a better smile. At least I don't look that old. She's such a ho/a prude/a square.

These types of comparisons muddy the waters when we examine our own reflections. We can't see ourselves clearly until we examine our own judgments and biases. There is no place where our own shit is more visible than when we are in intimate relationships with others.

As renowned feminist author bell hooks puts it, "The process begins with the individual woman's acceptance that American women, without exception, are socialized to be racist, classist and sexist, in varying degrees, and that labeling ourselves feminists does not change the fact that we must consciously work to rid ourselves of the legacy of negative socialization."[78] By delving into the judgments and biases of racism, classism, sexism, and homophobia, we can begin to peel off the masks we wear in order to find acceptance in our racist, classist, sexist, and homophobic cultures. True friendship is rooted in acceptance. It is a form of grassroots, organic feminism. It is an opportunity to learn the processes of empathy, compassion, patience, communication, and trust. It is a place to breathe, laugh, dance, think, and be.

We have friendships with men, too, and they are not inferior, but they are different. To expand on hooks's view, we believe men are also socialized in our innately sexist, patriarchal society, and in order to have true intimacy, they, too, must acknowledge the power differential they hold, even in friendships, and work consciously to understand their male privilege.

---

78. bell hooks, *Ain't I a Woman: Black Women and Feminism* (Cambridge, MA: South End Press, 1981).

The friendship between women can bring us, if we so desire, to the pool in order to examine our reflection and contemplate who we are in this world. In addition, true friendship can give us fuel for the journey to who we are becoming.

〜◎〜

Logically, there are huge implications when our value is defined externally. But the deepest damage is done when we begin to define and derive our own value through external sources. The consequences of making oneself into an object of external worth are tremendous. This is usually not apparent to us at first, because it is so incredibly common and more or less affects us all in some way; but for the person who has been exploited or abused sexually during childhood or adolescence, the value of the self becomes completely absorbed into the darkness of someone else's definition. The intimate bonds that we have with another are traumatic in origin. The boundaries of the self are permeable and safety is elusive. Multiple traumas easily occur because we have no gauge to know how to stop them, and often there is no responsible person present to stop trauma from occurring in the first place. The spirit is broken in early abuse, and as we noted in Chapter Two, the voice is lost. We become co-conspirators in our demise. The mind takes on the same dialogue, becoming perhaps even harsher than the original abusive voices, and we begin a journey of seeking approval (or disapproval), validation, and love from outside sources, as that is all we know and all that matters.

The concept of self-worth is difficult to understand because it has never been taught, and through all the early developmental stages we have been tainted by being an object of gratification or a narcissistic object for someone else. How could one possibly figure out how to love oneself when one has not been allowed to be a so-called "self," when one has been defined by another? There is no healthy model to return to, no healthy concept of sexuality to learn from, no sense of inherent value upon which to draw strength. This is precisely why the journey of healing childhood sexual trauma is so challenging, and why it requires such a long-term commitment to becoming whole.

The good news is that the human spirit is always striving in some way toward a place of wholeness, and, unless completely obliterated, it possesses a resilience that pushes onward despite the negative voices, the panic, the despair, the addictions, the depression, and inward demons of all shapes and sizes. The resilient spirit looks continually for the strategy, the plan, the way through, and it is this spirit in an individual that yearns for healing and never gives up. The individual may be lost, but the spirit continues to look for a way to be found. It is also the spirit within, the soul, the deep self—whatever you want to call it—that truly knows its original value and will not rest until we can see that value within ourselves. Thus begins the quest for healing and its gifts of light. It is the journey of ten million steps, some forward, some backward, and it is on this journey that we begin to learn to love ourselves from the inside out and begin not to define worth from the outside in.

The following story is about a young woman's need to find identity. As an abandoned child brought up by people unlike her, she found it necessary to separate and compartmentalize parts of her personality. Her experience is not unlike that of many who have been part of the child welfare system.

～ଡ଼ৎ

I've been a chameleon all my life. It's been easier that way. I've bent and molded myself to the desires of others from childhood on, and when that didn't work well, I constructed character images of myself that even I believed after some period of time. Some of those masks were dropped, of course—I could pass as a boy for only a short while, during adolescence, in my short haircut and boys' shirts and shorts. "Your grandson is so nice," a lady told my grandma. I felt proud. I'd achieved success in costuming.

There were other times later: creating the "bad girl" I became; preparing my mind to head off with the traveling-carnival crowd, not a care in the world; or even later, in New York City, wearing a scarf on my head, pretending not to be American. I could even look in the mirror and believe it was true. My face would change in expression and softness, and I would create some new image of me. Constructing images of the girl and the woman—not radical but comfortable images—to live under without fear of being known too deeply provide solace to the ones who find it unsafe or unkind to be themselves openly.

I especially trained myself well in listening to what men wanted, and for the men I loved or thought I loved, I tried to become all that they desired. Usually this failed, not because I wasn't successful, but because I was *too* successful and it grew easy for them to take me for granted. There was always a cost to my charades when they were over—an inner emptiness cowered under my solar plexus, completely bereft but held in stasis by a rock of weighted air. My form felt bent over, as if someone had punched me in the stomach. It was me holding my breath, me who knew the demons' names and was capable of being lost and, after a period of time, punishing myself without their help.

This became a habitual feeling, one that I hated but one that I knew, and it made it all the more clear that the next time I would have to make sure the image I portrayed was a little tighter and a little more distant. But the answer was not a newly constructed image, not a facade to hide behind or the familiarity of disguise. The answer, although it eluded me in so many ways after years of hiding, was in facing the real woman with all her secrets, her hidden-ness, her unknown parentage and history. I realized that I had to find a way to get to know her before she disappeared in her watery silence, leaving only the safety of created images, and me still a stranger to my deeper self.

It's impossible to know your purpose and live your path if you don't know who you really are or if you can't see your true beauty, strength, and resilience. It's equally impossible to find your true calling if you can't face the lurking shadows within. It's very scary, but necessary, to face shadows and see our true reflection. It isn't so ugly, is it?

Our minds are made up of many small dramas, traumas, and pain, but we are also equipped with all of the elements that support change and renewal at every stage of our living. We begin by glimpsing this possibility and not recoiling in fear, panic, or hate, and then, ever so slowly and with great patience, we reach out, sometimes on our knees, to the brilliant reflecting pool that shines back our own light. We figure out, rather slowly, how to befriend our minds and gain access to our hidden and hurting hearts—hearts that were broken long ago, before the mind was enlisted to create protection in whatever way it could.

As human beings, we hold the capacity for producing great light, as well as vast darkness. Narcissus saw his reflection in the water and believed that only his needs, his vision, and his reflection mattered. In doing so, he cut himself off from the bigger reality. Like one who tries to see with a blindfold or one eye covered, he missed much of the picture.

When we refuse to remove the blindfold from our eyes, we create more darkness for ourselves and others. When we give in to our fears or our lack of courage to face this darkness, we ironically become the monsters we seek to avoid. It is in our ability to face our reflections squarely and with compassion that we open ourselves to transformation, change, and inner freedom. What do we see in the reflected vision? How can we see what is reflected with courage and compassion? We look closely and kindly, without condemnation or criticism for all of our perceived failings and with thankfulness at all of our perceived gifts. We also look honestly at all the beauty and all the ugliness, knowing that neither defines us. In facing ourselves gently through our journaling, our art, our trusted friendships, and our most loved ones, we can dispel the monsters and no longer fear them. For it is in facing the monsters that we remove their hold on us. We find our deep inner power when we don't turn away from what threatens to destroy us. The monsters shrink and shrivel away when we stop giving them attention and hold them in compassionate disregard.

We can acknowledge our fears. We can overcome our places of darkness. There is a simple secret that we learn periodically and must remember again and again: real power and real strength come from within, and they are found within each of us if we mine them from the depths and treasure them as gold. It is this golden strength we need to see reflected in our eyes and the eyes of those we love. We all matter. We are all treasure. Once you know this, you will value the treasure in others, too.

CHAPTER 13

BREATHING AIR

No matter where you go, there you are.[79]

Our work over the years with young people and women has taught us many things, but we've also learned much about ourselves along the way. As with many "wounded healers," we chose professions that helped us make sense of our own erratic histories and troubled pasts. After all, those troubled times we faced were what led us to greater awakenings, making our lives more whole and balanced.

Sometimes the trauma narrative seems never-ending, particularly because early traumas are so often repeated for so many people. Most trauma survivors can relate to the pattern of breath-holding when upset, tense, or frightened. It becomes a way of life that is easy to revert to and remembered by the body. Even pain can begin to feel like a secure place to return to, and yet there is no healing in that pattern, just as there is no room for the deepened awareness of breath, moving through our bodies and clearing debris. Trauma survivors and those

---

79. Confucius quote, http://thinkexist.com/quotation/no_matter_where_you_go-there_you/185303.html.

who have endured deep marks on their souls have to begin to change their conscious relationship with their breath and their learned patterns of restricted breathing. It begins with a willingness to notice and be still. It also begins with an inhalation—so very simple. It begins the journey back into the body and begins showing us possibilities to know the truth of the heart. Air is funny like that—it opens us and creates room for expansion.

Most people habitually hold their breath, breathe shallowly, or constrict their breathing when fearful or in pain; however, this only worsens the symptoms and increases futile, frightened thinking. Old patterns and habits of mind keep us stuck in useless behaviors that become repetitive and too challenging to change. Finding a connection and a friendship with the breath helps calm the heart, bringing a person back into balance—even momentarily—as the body and the mind settle. Learning to breathe is usually the first thing we do after we are born and the last thing we give up when we die; so why, then, must we relearn it again and again throughout life? Because it is an automatic response, something we don't think of unless it is taken away, we take it for granted. If we've been afraid or made ourselves small in life, our breath reflects this choice and becomes more and more shallow. Learning to breathe again in new ways, with mindfulness and attention to the breath's ebb and flow, opens up new possibilities for addressing old patterns, facing fears, and feeling more awake and alive in our bodies and minds. It signifies to the body that healing is under way.

Learning new behaviors and how to be mindful and present is not the usual way for the majority of people, because it is so hard to change something that we thought protected us from fear, danger, and failure. Ironically, however, connection to the breath is what can actually help us overcome hardships and patterns that no longer serve us. Noticing and deepening the breath is what fully brings us back into our bodies and gives us the presence of mind to face the phantoms of fear, danger, pain, and perceived failures. It is our deeper, conscious breathing that creates the capacity to face all that we fear within ourselves, as well as in the outer world. If we learn to face the phantoms and demons within, then we can surely face anything on the outside. Nothing is more frightening than what we create in our minds, and so, with our breath, we can learn to know our minds, befriend the stalking tyrants of our thoughts that truly are our worst and most frightening foes, and achieve a connection of spirit and body that is accessible only when a person is calm and available. Our thoughts come and go, as do our emotions, and sometimes they cause us much upset, but using the breath as a means of reconnecting with a deeper source within ourselves enables us to move through any hardship of the mind with more presence and self-compassion.

Homeostasis is a state of equilibrium in the body that is maintained when tension or threat has been reduced. Dictionary .com defines homeostasis as "the tendency of a body to seek and maintain a condition of balance or equilibrium within its internal environment, even when faced with external changes."[80] For regular breath-holding, trauma-surviving worriers with numerous neurotic tendencies, this idea that the body seeks equilibrium, even when the mind is causing confusion, fear, or pain, is a great comfort. The fact that our body naturally tends to

80. Retrieved from: http://dictionary.reference.com/browse/homeostasis?s=t

want to stabilize shows us that we can rely on something other than our minds to bring us into balance. Therefore, homeostasis can become a guide that eventually teaches us about the power of the breath and its ability to bring us even greater equilibrium, as well as providing a presence of mind that in turn creates pathways that allow us to feel our emotions and move through them with some integrity. Homeostasis can be a marvelous thing to remember and rely upon during challenging times. It's good to know that our bodies and minds seek balance even when we don't know how.

The Greek word *pneuma* means "breath" and also "spirit." "Spirit" in Latin is *spiritus* and also means "breath." In the context of this discussion, we use the word "spirit" to refer to the noncorporeal substance that dwells within us and gives us life. It is often understood as our consciousness and as the part of us that remains past death. It leaves us when the breath leaves us, and so it has become synonymous with that part of us that survives after our bodies die. Once spirit—or breath—is gone from the body, the body is only an empty shell. Connecting to breath within us and learning to calm ourselves in the midst of chaos is humans' lifelong way of accessing the spirit and essence within us. This connection is part of solving the riddles the mind creates.

Yogis and Zen masters have known for thousands of years about our capacity to heal our minds and our deepest hurts by becoming aware and working with our breathing, but in our frantic, anxiety-driven world, we run from stillness and remain in discomfort. We have forgotten how to use the power within us, as it is easier to forget our pain by reaching for a drug or a drink, or for sex, or for some other fix. It has always been easier to run than to face the mind squarely, and that is why it is unusual and much more difficult to choose consciousness. As Adrienne Rich said, "Every act of becoming conscious is an unnatural act."[81]

Ultimately, however, the habits of mind that we have cultivated as individuals and as a society to avoid all that creates pain and suffering only induce more suffering, and we become like a cat chasing its tail. Yet freedom comes only in facing the mind's tyrants, the old wounds, the habits that keep us stuck in patterns of misery and despair—the very pain that we often seek to avoid. Our breath is the vehicle that assists us in the process of traveling through this difficult terrain. It will not fail us. It is our steadfast ally like no other. It is the beginning point, but also, when we work with it over time, it becomes a place to return to again and again to find comfort and strength. We breathe air, we breathe life in, and with a little intention we begin to reclaim our selves and our voice. Finding healing is a lengthy process that requires a strong and willing internal spirit, but as we inhale it in, it carries us forward with every exhalation.

The next story is about a woman who taught herself to breathe through her suffering and to emerge on the other side into a place of self-love. Experiencing compassion for herself was difficult at first, but it was the beginning of the bigger changes that followed.

---

81. Retrieved from: http://www.solidarity-us.org/node/3684

Her dark brown eyes searched mine for a semblance of hope.

I smiled at her frown. "Just breathe," I said, "for one minute. You can do it."

She closed her eyes—to block me out, maybe, or maybe to concentrate on her breath. We had discussed this before, had sat in the dark together, just the two of us, breathing in the midnight hour. The look on her face was one of total concentration. In silence, I willed her on. *Just breathe*, I thought, not saying a word.

She breathed in through her nose. The air was moist and warm. I breathed in with her; I could smell the fragrance in the air: a citrusy vanilla. I closed my eyes as well and imagined the sweet smell of the Holy Spirit, the aroma of God floating past me. I inhaled the power, the essence of life, the strength of the divine. She breathed out, and I felt her breath—we were that close. I could hear her heartbeat as she willed it to slow down. Her hands were clenched and sweaty, and she uncurled her fingers as she breathed in again; her shoulders drooped, and the warm air ran through her body to her toes. Her eyes were still closed, but I opened mine so I could watch her. I loved this woman, although most times she didn't know it. I knew I didn't always put her first, but I longed to learn. I closed my eyes again, quickly. Tears began to form on my eyelids, cold tears of sadness and regret. They would not fall—I would not allow them. No more regret, no more sadness. I inhaled, as did she.

"Breathe," I whispered. "Almost there, just a minute." I knew how hard this minute would be. The world was ending all around us; the wounds felt fatal and the fear intense. "If you can just get through this minute," I murmured, "you can get through the next."

"Minute by minute," she uttered softly. We had shared this moment before. I opened my eyes and studied her face. I hadn't always thought she was beautiful but had slowly, over time, learned how to revere her face: her honey-brown skin, her perfect full lips, the way her eyes turned up at the corners and wrinkled when she smiled, the deep line furrowing her brow when she was afraid. The acne scars, a remnant of a stressful time, visible when you looked closely. Breathe. We breathed, together, and slowly our heartbeats became one. Minute by minute, we would get through the day together.

She opened her eyes. Our minute was up. I reached out to touch her face.

The mirror was cold and fogged now because of my misty breath. I wiped the glass and smiled again at my reflection. It smiled back. Sometimes that was all I had: myself and my breath. But it was a start. Minute by minute.

Over the years, we have worked with many children and youth in the child welfare system, including children in foster care, detention, group homes, psychiatric institutions, and schools. We have had the opportunity to be there for many children when family and/or the system failed them. These are opportunities we have not taken lightly, as we know young life needs to be cherished and valued and we believe that we need to increase the capacity to assist children in need everywhere.

So many children have challenged beginnings. Adoption, maternal deprivation, and foster care are a few of the ways in which children lose a connection to themselves. But if these children's feelings and needs are respected, then they can deal constructively with those early disconnected emotions and feelings of abandonment. Unfortunately, many do not address these feelings and needs early on and must thus reconcile them in some manner later in life. Therapy, as well as other holistic healing modalities we have mentioned—such as art, movement, music, acupuncture, and yoga—can be extremely beneficial. If people don't address what ails them from deep within, then they are often resigned to repeating the same non-constructive patterns over and over again. The next piece is about someone who attempted to find her way as an adult while making room to heal childhood wounds.

She was born with a heart. In that heart were tunnels and places of blood, pulsation, and strength. In that heart were the makings of every heart that comes into being on this planet: ventricles and valves, passages and blood, like ocean waves rushing forth with force, coming and going like an interior tide—the waves of the sea that flows through all who breathe. Coming into the world, we are all born with our hearts, but physically and metaphorically the nature of being a human being is that hearts break, shrink, shatter, expand (and open again, too) many times over a lifetime. However, when the heart of a young child experiences shattering, it is unlikely ever to be whole or fully healthy again. Of course, the process of healing must be embraced, but to be fully healed remains an individual question and a challenge.

It remained a question for the little girl, too, for she was aware that she had a secret that she had to keep in order to protect other people, even though, because of that secret, she herself would have to suffer for the sake of others. This one came into the world to a mother who was unconscious at her birth and consequently remained unconscious to the girl for all of her life.

Several days after her birth, the girl was taken away and given to a family that wanted a child. At that point, her identity became no longer her own but defined by circumstances. It was always her suspicion that those early days alone must have caused something in her heart to change immediately, because on a very deep level she learned there was no one to count on, no one to trust. There was no mother, no love at birth, no tenderness, so by the time she went to her new family, she was already afraid. But these things were not recognized back then, and no one would have believed her.

There are many small deaths along the way of living. The letting go doesn't come easily. The losses that feel fatal and the good-byes that sound futile seemingly indicate an ending worse than death and more like oblivion. At least, that was how it felt to the little girl. Her life on Earth began with a good-bye to her mother. Those first breaths came, and she was lost to the one who carried her to the shores of life. In the bright lights of a hospital room, harsh words were spoken and a woman, just barely a mother, buried her feelings in shame and denial.

It was probably how she survived. But the little girl became human, alive in the world, a baby and at once an old being, disconnected from all that felt safe and secure. This, she carried through life as pattern and protection.

There are many others like her, whose earliest memories of pain and abandonment cannot be rewritten. It happens not only to the adopted but also to those abandoned at birth because of multitudes of other factors: drugs, illicit relationships, sexual abuse, poverty, and other unresolved traumas. No matter, though—the end result is an untethered existence that longs for connection. Some may find it; others search for it endlessly, through bad relationships and unhealthy partners, abuse and violence, and a learned numbing of residual pain. They run toward hope and then run away just as quickly, crumbling on the path and feeling forgotten.

This was what she came to know, and she was not alone. Her loneliness was an abusive companion for many years, but one day it became her fierceness and her strength. It was then that loneliness changed and became solitude, and it made her strong, compassionate, and unable to be defeated by circumstance. One day, she returned to her breath and she learned to float on it like a life raft.

At first, the life raft was shaky and not trustworthy, but in time and with practice, she gained the skills to maneuver it and learned to sail.

It's a process to trust the instincts and rhythms that lie inside us, because we are all so conditioned to look for the answers outside ourselves. But what is broken within us can be fixed only within us. The resources available to us may be hidden, but in the recesses of the heart lie the answers we need. We get to the dark places of pain, the broken promises, and the old, old hurts by setting forth on the life raft of the breath.

And that is how the little girl began to heal.

At the end of a yoga class, the participants roll onto their right sides and curl into a fetal position with their arms folded underneath their heads. The lights of the room are dim, and the light from the day is fading. A sliver of moon is suspended and visible through the big, steamy windows. They end the class in *savasana*, the pose of the corpse. It is said that this pose of surrender integrates the benefits of a yoga practice into the body and mind. The practitioners let go of their attention on breath and movement and relax all the muscles, slowly releasing their bodies onto the mats. It is often said that this is the most difficult yoga posture because it is not about doing anything besides simply lying still on the floor.

Yoga has become very popular in the United States in recent decades, but it has been practiced throughout the world for hundreds of years. Yoga is the connecting of body and mind through a series of practices that include physical movement, meditation, breathing, and self-discipline. The practice is thought to have emerged in pre-Vedic India; the early writings of Patanjali, an Indian master, explain the benefits and purposes of yoga from that time. These writings have been translated from the original Sanskrit into English by several scholars in order that we might understand this ancient wisdom, which remains relevant today.

Like many ancient spiritual writings, the yoga sutras teach the process of becoming whole through meditation, overcoming obstacles, dealing with pain, and living a fuller, richer life through self-awareness and internal discipline. They also point to the importance of learning how to breathe. The breath is said to be linked to our thoughts and connected to "the inner winds."[82] Practitioners are encouraged to "keep a close eye"[83] on the breath, both during exercise and throughout the day. The sutras note that inhalations occur much more quickly than exhalations when a person is upset or nervous, and that practitioners can correct this issue by mentally counting, second by second, the duration of each inhalation and exhalation to make sure they are equal in length. These ancient teachings are completely in line with what yogis and meditation experts encourage today.

The exercises and attention to breathing in yoga are called *pranayama*. *Prana* is the vital air of the body found in the act of respiration and also in the fluids of the body, including blood, vaginal fluids, and semen. The latter part of the word—*ayama*— has to do with the length or suspension of the breath. *Pranayama* is often practiced in modern-day yoga classes as a means of deepening the physical practice and strengthening the body, and, like other practices of working with the breath, it can have a profound effect on stress levels and practitioners' coping skills.

Yoga can give us so much, and not just *asana*, the physical practice of poses that expand our bodily awareness and increase our strength—although that is a good beginning. Yoga also offers us a chance to examine our minds, to practice doing no harm outwardly or inwardly, to learn to meditate, to gain

82. Michael Roach Geshe and Christie McNally, "How to Breathe," in *The Essential Yoga Sutra* (New York: Doubleday, 2005).
83. Ibid.

awareness about where our minds go when we're not paying attention, and to learn to be free and unencumbered in body, mind, and spirit.

All physical activity helps us to stay connected to our bodies and to integrate all aspects of our embodied selves more fully, but yoga points the way through unification of breath and movement in a way that is more intentional than other forms of exercise. Integrating body, mind, and spirit opens up places within in which movement of matter, thought, and emotion can occur more readily. This discipline, this "practice," teaches us new things about ourselves and our reactions all the time. It teaches us to be still when things crumble or fall apart, as they are apt to do. Our bodies and our minds change on a daily basis, but the more we work with them, the greater sense of control and connection we can cultivate. Yoga can teach us to be more patient, more willing.

The *Bhagavad Gita*, another great, time-tested guidebook and resource on understanding the depth of a true yoga practice, offers instruction through the story of Krishna and Arjuna. This book from Indian culture has informed the work of Mahatma Gandhi and many others over countless generations. Among its offerings of wisdom, it instructs that challenges are sometimes our greatest teachers. Its words can comfort and encourage us. "On this path effort never goes to waste, and there is no failure. Even a little effort toward spiritual awareness will protect you from the greatest fear."[84]

---

84. *The Bhagavad Gita*, trans. Eknath Easwaran (Tomales, CA: Nilgiri Press, 1985), 93.

While we are healing from trauma, it is critical for us to be in touch with the needs and experiences of our body. Beyond yoga, other physical activity—such as running, dance, sports, or working out at a gym—can also be instrumental. If there is an activity that calls to you or makes you feel fully alive and in your body, then that is a good activity to practice in your life. Being disconnected from our bodies and our breathing is a clear sign of being deeply affected by trauma or post-traumatic stress symptoms. Finding a rejuvenating physical activity is a means of reestablishing that internal connection. Being comfortable in the body will help as you work with your mind. If physical activity is not an option, working with a personal trainer, a physical therapist, or a body worker can also help you reconnect with the body.

Finding ways to reconnect with the mind is similarly imperative. For people who have constant pain, the practice of mindfulness can help them deal with both physical and emotional pain. Mindfulness is moment-to-moment awareness practiced in a nonjudgmental manner, and a means of giving the mind space to interpret experiences in different ways than habitual thinking patterns allow. This practice is being utilized more and more in health care settings and in mental health therapy, especially to break cycles of anxiety and fear and old patterns of trauma in the body.

Peter Levine, PhD, author of *Waking the Tiger* and founder of a form of therapy called "somatic experiencing," has pioneered much of the work on mindfulness as a form of healing.[85] Levine believes that trauma is an activated, incomplete biological response to a threat, and that incomplete response has become frozen or fixed in time. When humans are unable

---

85. Peter A. Levine, *Waking the Tiger: Healing Trauma* (Berkeley, CA: North Atlantic Books, 1997).

to discharge the energy they feel when the defense mechanism of fight, flight, or freeze kicks in, that undischarged energy gets locked into patterns within the neuromuscular system that create chronic arousal, stress, and bodily dysfunction. These patterns can show up in a variety of ways, including panic attacks, chronic anxiety, gastrointestinal issues, stress disorders, and headaches, to name only a few. Levine believes that traumatized people become fixated in an aroused state that makes normal functioning increasingly difficult.

In *Waking the Tiger*, he notes that animals are able to complete their biological response to threat by rolling in the grass, physically shaking their bodies, or sweating and shivering. Humans also have the capacity to shake off their biological response to threat, but doing so is not generally encouraged after a traumatic event. Sometimes after a scare or a shock, we might find ourselves shivering and shaking like animals do. The usual response is to cover the person with a blanket to eliminate the shivering response, when in actuality, according to Levine and others who have researched somatic experiencing, it would be better to allow the body to complete the biological response and to return to its natural state of equilibrium on its own (the wonders of homeostasis again!).

We are alive as long as we breathe. Keep breathing and coming back to that vital life force that courses through your veins, no matter what. Know that your connections to yourself are symbolic of greater connections to the world around you. Celebrate them, love them, honor them, and acknowledge their strength within you. As long as there is breath in your body, there is possibility for change and renewal.

Learning that we can withstand the challenges that we face with grace and a tenacity of spirit is essential to our healing journey. Our next story illuminates the magic of the world just beyond our everyday knowledge—a place that can help us tap into great internal strength if we just open our vision to the possibilities.

The woman who lives alone burns a candle on this early-winter night and watches waves and sea and spinning currents of air. Standing with her body pressed against the balcony rail, her nightgown and shawl blowing back, she leans forward into the wind as a figurehead on an old sailing ship. She has a strong and fragile heart. The only way through the land mines of heartache as a constantly recurring pattern and theme, a danger she can't seem to get past, has been to come to this place at the edge of land and sky and lean into the familiar fear, lean into wind. Where has she experienced this before? She does not remember now, but she knows this with a familiarity. Lean into the wind, and trust that it will hold the weight of your body in flight.

The waves are crazy tonight. They break so far out, and then again, and so much white water moves all the way to the shore from the faraway breaks. Sometimes they rip like lightning across the face of the sea—a water-and-light show of the earth. The moon, on its first night after fullness, is just beginning its waning course, making the ocean alive with light even on a cloudy night. *La mère*, a feminine force that is all things unfeminine in this culture—strong, unknown, life-renewing, life-taking, ever free and unharnessed, and constant—is also the home of the underworld and original mystery.

The woman who lives alone feels the force of the night wind holding her body as it would a bird.

"Where are the heroines I can follow?" the woman asks the sea.

It is listening but does not answer.

"How do we love another fully and honor our own hearts?" she continues. "How do we still love deeply when we have experienced such hurt at the hands of others who have not truly loved us? How do we carry on? How do we find the strength to love within ourselves?"

The winds carry the cries of her ravaged heart to the ocean depths, and the sea replies, "Remain strong, dear woman, and trust the current on which you rest your body. Lean into its force. Breathe it in, and trust it will not fail you."

"But where are the heroines of this time? Where are the women to show the way back to our sacred shores of heart, heat, sexuality, and an embodied life?"

The ocean screams out, as she knows this pain all too well. There have been too many centuries of disregard for her precious body, so many shades of blue and green. Alone, she knows not the answers; she must summon the depths and the ones who reside within them.

"Where are the heroines to show the way?" repeats the woman.

And from the cascading spray of cresting white waves, Aphrodite and her siren companions emerge in their undying fortitude and immortal beauty. Like Venus, like true love, like all power that is real and of another world, they return the call.

"Become them! Become them!"

Become the heroines? the woman wonders. *But how?*

"Become them," they repeat, and as quickly as they appeared, they are gone on the wind under layers of sea spray.

The woman returns to her bed alone but not lonely. Lovers, fathers of children, husbands, partners, one-night stands, dispassionate fools, impostors and abusers of love have passed through her life, and there will be others, perhaps a more worthy one to call her mate of soul—one who will know the value of her love and cherish her heart as his own. But for now, there is breath and body and wind and time to become the heroine she was born to be.

CHAPTER 14

THE SACRED HEART

And then a strange thing happened. For where the tear had fallen a flower grew out of the ground, a mysterious flower, not at all like any that grew in the garden.[86]

This is for all of the once-ugly girls with knotty, unruly hair, always cut too short and never quite behaving. The little girls who wished to be boys for the freedom they had and the different air they somehow got to breathe. Little girls who saw no one stand up for them, but knew that, like their hair, they had to stand up, so they did. They stood up and got in trouble constantly for being incorrigible, undisciplined, untrained. This is for the little girls who were never ugly but felt so ugly that they acted that way, to claim the ugly as their own and cover up the ugly that had never really been there on the surface but bubbled and simmered below, seasoned by the ugly words they couldn't get out of their heads.

This is for the little girls who held the hand of shame tight-

---

86. Margery Williams, *The Velveteen Rabbit* (New York: Doubleday, 1922), 26.

ly and didn't let go, even when it squeezed back too tightly and hurt them badly. Like an abusive partner, the shame became a familiar friend, one they couldn't turn their backs on, for they had been through too much together. It was the shame that held them in the night and apologized for being so horrible; it was the shame that promised never to do it again and never to leave. Even though the little girls squeezed their eyes shut and willed it gone, when they opened their eyes again, it was still there, smiling, with yellow teeth and a crooked grin.

This is for the little girls who began to grow up, their figures changed and their souls grown wise, often before their time. They longed for love and found it deep within their own hearts. They wondered, when they were alone at night, whether the strange bedfellows would be there in the morning. Shame left eventually, not by choice, but because the little girls packed their bags and moved away, leaving him standing there alone with no one to torment. The little girls missed his whispers. At first they would whisper to themselves, mimicking his voice, until they remembered why they had left in the first place. They learned how to breathe. They learned how to be still and listen, not to shame but to the unfamiliar voice of their own hearts. Like the still-small voice of God, their hearts whispered, and they listened. They laughed at some of the things their hearts said, not the high, shrill laugh of those who taunted and teased, but the soft chuckle of best friends, a contagious giggle that began deep in their toes and traveled like a streetcar in and out of traffic, all the way up to the tips of their ears.

Some of the things their hearts said made them cry. But the little girls learned to embrace their tears; they licked the moisture from the top of their lips as though they tasted the salty spray of the ocean. They sometimes had to hold their hearts, cupping their dreams and desires in their hands like a wounded bird who had fallen from her nest. They blew hot air into their hearts as though they were warming cold hands on a winter's night, thawing out the frozen pieces of their broken hearts, until the hearts began to beat again with the familiar beat of ancient drums. The hearts kept the rhythm, and the girls smiled. They weren't children anymore; they were women, wise, astute, and nurturing, full of love. They still misbehaved, but now they weren't always afraid; they were proud of their boldness, and they kept moving forward, sometimes taking giant steps, sometimes pixie steps, like childhood games. Sometimes they skipped, and at times, when they were in great pain, they crawled, but they never stopped moving. They never stopped weeping, they never stopped laughing; they embraced the act of living in all its terror and all its joy. All of it, this entire journey, had become a part of them. The beauty and the ugliness had become part of who they were. And that was okay.

As we describe the difficult journey we have taken, the narrative of many women before us, and many still to come, we paint a picture of hope, an image of hearts mending and lives fusing together, a glimpse of faith into what may be now or may be coming soon. We are tired; many times, breathing may be all that we have had the energy to do. Yet we have become warriors. We have a resilience that can be conceived only at the onset of trauma and birthed in the struggle of life. Our scars remind us of all that we have endured. We have tried many things to help us find our way. We write hoping you will try many things, too. We have not given up, and we hope that you will not give up either.

Often the steps toward healing are as medicinal as the healing itself. There are victories along the way, medals one obtains, that are not easily come by. You may wear them around your neck or on your breastplate, silently yet proudly showing them off to others. You may place them carefully in a wooden box lined with red velvet, like a medal of honor from a forgotten war. You may overlook the trauma you have endured, until someone notices it tucked away, dusty with age, and gently asks you to share the secrets of your heart. The trauma may remain part of your every day, hanging on your leg like a screaming child, one you try to soothe and silent but who has a mind of her own and will not be stopped. You may remove your mask at times, or at least peek out from behind it, wondering whether the joys of life have really invited you to the party. Still, you walk in the door and show up. Still, you are here and the medals you have earned are yours to keep and cherish.

You must also remember that you are not alone. There are others. There are women who have endured unspeakable things. You may meet them in a group or lock eyes across a crowded room. The mask they wear may hide their past, but you recognize the pain behind their smile. They, like you, are gentle warriors, and although they don't quite know how, they may long to connect with similar souls. They know they cannot go alone, yet they know betrayal, too, so it is difficult to trust.

They may lash out in anger, roll their eyes at you, forge ahead with no regard for human casualties, but, like a secret password to an underground club, your scars remind each other that you are one and the same: *You belong outside, and you will find air and freedom out here. You belong, outsider.*

It is okay to smile, to speak, to share, to love, to trust. Although of course doing so is not easy, each time you try will become a new victory, offering you mementos of risks taken and conquests achieved. Again, wholeness is not merely a destination; it is a journey, too.

The warrior is a helpful metaphor for women on the path to health or to becoming healers in their own right. For those who have lived on the fringes, the warrior is often their embodied way of surviving in this world. The cruelty that so many women have faced in their lives requires a warrior's heart to endure. In our own lives, we have found the spirit and the value of the warrior within us. The next story is about one such woman's journey.

The warrior is resilient and brave; she stands upright at the edge of the cliff, assessing the valley below. She is beautiful, confident, and aware. Education has empowered her; she has studied her path and become familiar with her enemies. She is alert; her senses are heightened, and they work in unison to notice every movement, every smell, every sound, every threat, every opening. Joy bubbles within her. Even her soul is excited about this journey. She has direction and purpose, although it is not hers alone; she answers to a purpose greater than herself. A warrior would be a fool to go into battle alone. She has trusted advisors and seeks wise counsel from within and without. Every failed battle strengthens her to win the war.

Her shield is her faith. It was heavy at first, but she has learned how to maneuver it and she trusts its protection. She exercises with her shield each day. As if she were doing the beautiful dance of t'ai chi, she stands in the cove of trees in the early-morning sunlight and allows the skill of faith to be sharpened. The sun, like warm honey, drips a golden hue around about her body.

Her helmet is her salvation. It covers her head, drapes her shoulders, and protects and salves the wounds of the past. Her eyes are visible, dark and mysterious, piercing all they gaze upon. They have seen too much, those eyes, but they have not become hardened. They are still so open, searching, assessing, longing, and yet completely satisfied by what they see. They light up as she chuckles to herself, and the corners crease, revealing for a moment her age and wisdom.

Her breastplate is righteousness, guarding her heart. She hasn't always worn her armor. Her breasts are scarred and her heart has been broken, but the scars have become a source of beauty, like an intricate henna tattoo decorating her golden-brown skin. The breastplate is jeweled, a complex mosaic; she is proud to wear it. She is indignant about the mistreatment of others for personal gain. She is indignant because of the cruelty she has witnessed.

Her loins are girded with the belt of truth. It hangs low on her hips, accentuating the curves of her femininity. She has learned not only to follow truth but to use it. Assessing daily what tools she will need, she attaches them to the hooks on her belt. These tools of truth will make her journey easier. Her thighs are thick and strong, her calves robust, her boots laced tight yet her feet spread the gospel of peace, not war, in every direction that she walks. To fight is easy; to restrain takes bravery. She is a conqueror, a gentle warrior, and with peace at her feet she can walk for miles.

Her sword is her only weapon, the word of her God, sharper than any two-edged sword, piercing and dividing marrow from bone. She uses it mostly for food, so she and her family can be replenished, but in battle she will draw it. With precision and accuracy, she will slay the enemy. This truth is unconquerable.

After a while the warrior moves, returning to camp to gather those she must protect. She has mapped out her journey in part and is ready to begin. Nothing will stop her from reaching her destination. Nothing will stop her from being victorious; she may not know the whole route, but in faith she trusts and she will find her way. She understands the beauty in the journey. When she gathers her children around the fire late at night, she knows she will relay to them the stories of battle. They will listen and learn, and her lessons will make their walk a little easier. There is no right way, she will tell them—every path they choose will have a lesson of its own; every step will prepare them for what is to come. But to win, to overcome, one must begin the journey.

Ancient thinkers, including Aristotle, believed that the seat of consciousness resided in the heart and not the head. This, of course, has changed over time as scientists have learned more about the brain. Today, however, we still do not really know where our consciousness resides. We do know that we feel with the heart center of our body. When we love someone deeply and learn that love over time and through trial, it changes us and it changes our hearts. Our hearts have the ability to feel vast and expansive in deep love. The ancient Greeks had names for four different types of love, including romantic love, spiritual love, the love of deep but nonsexual affection, and love between friends and families. In all of these situations, our hearts can be devastated and broken.

In women who have endured sexual trauma at an early age, the ability to engage in all of these types of love—especially romantic and sexual love—may be challenged. Wounded women know the pain of the broken heart profoundly within their being. The choice for all of us is to honor the breaking open of the heart, and either to become a "wounded healer"[87] in the world or to operate from a place of woundedness, thus wounding others in our paths out of our own brokenness. It takes great courage to love well in this world. It takes great courage to stand in the force of the heart.

The following story is about one woman's quest of the heart.

---

87. A term coined by Carl Jung (see http://en.wikipedia.org/wiki/Wounded_healer).

The giving of the heart is a dangerous and revolutionary act. Aphrodite knew this and had warned the woman ahead of time. In fact, it was Aphrodite who said, "Play awhile more, take a lover, tarry here momentarily and enjoy this man's lusciousness and the joy he brings to you, but do not stay and do not let him have your heart!"

But it had been a long time since someone had loved the woman, and he surely did. He took his time with her, understanding that she did not trust him at first and was skeptical to let him into her house. He didn't mind. He was patient and kept coming back. He waited on the porch, and when she let him in, he handed her a rose and smiled. Later, he did the dishes, too. The woman was amused and pleased. She let him into her bed one night, and he tossed and turned her like a ship on a wild sea, perilous indeed but so very exciting. This became a trip she took often, ignoring the warnings from the shore: the dimming of the lighthouse beams and the distancing of the foghorns as she moved out farther and farther into unpredictable high seas.

In time, they moved away from land entirely and resided on a distant island during their moments together. He took her hands in his and kissed her forehead; they prayed together, danced together, loved deeply, talked of many and any things. He did not want anyone else, and he would not let her go. He asked her to stay with him and love him. She said yes.

That was about the time that she took her heart from her chest and showed it to him: pulsating, precious red with golden beams. She shared it with him and let him hold it, kiss it. Her heart, very scared, prayed fervently that it was valued and that in his strong and callused yet gentle hands it would not be dropped onto the ground and shattered.

Romantics and mystics do not live in linear time, and neither do hearts, so when she shared it with him, a little part stayed in his hands and did not come back to her. That little part, made up of all the same cells as her heart, jumped into his chest eagerly and snuggled up alongside the heart that belonged to him. This was risky business for a skeptical chick, but she was learning to trust. One time, lying in bed, touching heart to heart and face to face, she sensed a warm glow between their bodies and then felt a circle of gold like a halo bonding their bodies through the hearts. It lasted minutes and was unflinching. While the man and woman were amazed and awed by the strength and presence of this love, their hearts were delighted but not surprised. The woman whispered aloud the words "I trust you," just to see how it felt.

And so it went on for some time, but the woman remained afraid each day that he would leave her. Patterns of the past always foretold that loving cannot endure and someone has to "exit stage left" at the end of Act One, never to return. Old voices from the balcony screamed at her: *Unworthy! Not beautiful! Too old! Too intense! Not enough, not invited! You don't BELONG!* And then the skeptical voices: *He's an impostor and a liar! You've been duped! Stupid! He never loved you, ever—he's this way with every woman, don't you know? Stupid you! Bullshit man!*

Fuck you! she screamed back, but the voices secretly worried her.

And so she became more afraid of him and how he could

hurt her, and her fear became even more prevalent as he became distracted by his past and began to show serious signs of ambivalence and inconsistency. The more distracted he became, the more she moved into the habitation of fear. It became hurtful to her heart, which wanted only to love without drama.

"He is emotionally dangerous," said the woman next door. "Get a horse and ride away fast."

"I can't afford a horse right now," answered the woman.

"You can't afford him, either," replied the neighbor.

One day the thing she feared came to pass, and it was almost a relief. *Thank God he left me; now I don't have to worry about that anymore.* So she walked once again to the land of love lost, to the deep green and gray colors of the desert, filled with the scent of the creosote bush, and looked inward at what dwelled there. Such an eager and hopeful heart remained; like a patient, magical being it sat, still and fierce, resolving not to close off, not to forget, not to give up hope, ever.

She smiled reluctantly. She had learned from this heart—so strong, fierce, and real—to be her true self, and no man, no unworthy heart, no false or true love, could throw her off track. For where the strong and willing heart reigns, deep love endures and divine love dwells.

The woman called to Aphrodite for guidance. Aphrodite smiled and said, "No love is ever wasted. Seeking pleasure for pleasure's sake is one thing, but who would ever think that one could love so deeply and never feel pain? But there is no reason to fear or suffer, for love, like all energy, is not destroyed but only transformed. You must simply trust what I tell you, and your heart . . . well, as for the heart, you must celebrate her strength."

Aphrodite turned to go, and then, looking back toward the woman, she stopped. Like Botticelli's Venus, replete with beauty, sensuality, and the power of self-knowledge, she said, "Honor your courageous heart, sister, and she will lead you well for all of your days and beyond."

It takes good courage to love true and well, and the heart knows such things. The woman could go back to hiding or she could freeze until bitterness prevailed; she could cry until the tears no longer came or she could let it all pass through her with curiosity and kindness and dust herself off again.

"What did we learn?" asked the woman of her heart.

"We are brave and true," replied her heart, "but mostly we know that real love has no end and is never lost. To lose ourselves in fear is not to trust this profound truth. Where fear rules, love cannot prevail and the presence of the moment is obscured."

And together, the woman and her heart began to learn to trust the mysteries that would continually unfold as long as they remained open to the possibilities created by living fully.

Learning to stay present in the face of pain, hurt, and betrayal is extraordinarily difficult and unpleasant, but its rewards are numerous. Our dominant culture encourages us to run away from ourselves, to avoid pain, and to blame ourselves and others, instead of experiencing defeat, accepting pain, and creating new pathways. The following conversation took place one evening in one of our girls' groups.

∽⟨֎⟩∽

"I am going to stay," she said definitively. She wasn't smiling, although she didn't appear cross, either. She seemed very certain.

"Stay?" one of the girls asked her. "What, stay *here*? That ain't a goal; your ass ain't goin' nowhere, no way!"

The girls laughed. She wasn't agitated; she simply repeated, even more determinedly, "I am going to stay. When I want to run, I am going to stay." She held up her journal; she had written "STAY" in capital letters, bold, sturdy, almost unmovable: STAY.

"I never stay," she said, looking down, "whenever things get hard, either in my group home or at home with my mom. It don't matter the situation—if shit got hard, I was outta there. I lived on an AWOL. I was AWOL from my own life. Now, I am going to *stay*."

On the way home, the two of us spoke about some of the times when we had run in our own lives—run from or to relationships, run away from home or from ourselves. Too much running had occurred in our lives. Later that evening, Stacey told of the following experience.

I contemplated her words as I lay in the bath. I closed my eyes and submerged my head under the warm bubbles. I ran my hands through my hair and felt the steamy water fill my ears. I listened to the sound of nothing as it rang through my head. I opened my heart and saw a little girl running. She was running faster than she had ever run before; her limbs were long and her strides were wide. She was barefoot and felt the grass under her feet. The field ahead would be her refuge. It was a cornfield, its large, golden stalks sown in neat, linear furrows eight to ten inches apart, just wide enough for her to squeeze her body through.

She didn't look back. She instinctively knew if she turned her head, it might slow her down. But she also knew no one was following her. They never did. They always continued their lives as though she didn't exist. When it became dusk and she crept home, exhausted from running and crying, they wouldn't even look up from whatever it was they were doing. She knew they heard her, but they went on, as did life.

When you run and no one comes to find you, you keep running anyway. You never really know if you are running from or running to, but you just keep running.

I lifted my head from the water and rested it on the edge of the tub. I noticed the coldness of the porcelain in contrast with the warmth of the water.

When the little girl stopped running, she walked instead, her bare feet finding soft spots of soil on which to step. She weaved in and out of the corn stalks. It wasn't enough to run; she also knew she had to hide. When she was sufficiently concealed in the middle of the field, she sat down. Pulling her knees to her body, she buried her head in her lap. She thought if she made herself really, really small, even if they looked, they wouldn't find her. She felt herself shrinking, smaller and smaller and smaller, like a character from *The Borrowers*. So small, she was no longer important, no longer necessary, no longer noticed. She stayed there, a small girl in a big field, until the darkness started to fall. Then, as quietly as she had entered, she tiptoed home.

I ran my hands down my body, lathering my skin with sweet-smelling soap. I thought of all the times I had run. I ran from pain and I ran from love. It may have seemed as if I stayed; they may not have even noticed I was gone, because I wore the mask of presence, but I was really running, farther and farther away, deep into the cornfields. I washed my breasts and thought of all the times I ran from love, not just emotional love but true intimacy. Sex had become fear inducing; when it was just "sex," it was not scary, it was an occupation, a chore, but when it became linked with my soul and began to penetrate my heart, it awakened a carnal fear, a fear of abandonment, of rejection, of loss, of not being good enough. It became a self-fulfilling prophecy, almost: I ran, they left, I was alone.

The key for those of us who have experienced trauma is learning how to stay, learning how to be present in our bodies, present in our hearts, present in our lives. I massaged my belly and thought of the strength of my womb, the children conceived within my midst. I thought of the flutters of life I had felt that I hadn't been able to run from. I thought of the core of my being, the excitement that dwelled there when I found love, the fear that hid there when I could no longer run. I washed between my legs, the very center of my sexuality, the birthplace of life and the source of so much pleasure and pain. I thought of the men who had visited there and never known its worth, my worth. I thought of the sacredness of my vulva and the unspeakable force that resided deep within my vagina. I wondered if I had the power to truly stay. Could I allow the joys and sensuality of love to be rebirthed in this place of nativity?

I ran my hands down my thighs to the tips of my toes and re-membered those bare feet that ran so far away and so long ago. It was time to stop running. I had to learn how to stay, how to trust, how to let go. My feet needed to walk the unfamiliar path of forgiving the unforgiveable. The path of forgiveness could not be run; it was too steep and full of briars and thorns. I could walk it, though; sometimes that would mean going backward, to the place where the pain lived, but not always. Sometimes it would mean forging ahead, reaching forward toward the peace, grabbing the peace with my hands and refusing to let it go.

I lifted my hands out of the water. Hands that had held, nurtured, slapped, scrubbed, caressed; tiny little-girl hands that swung by my side as I walked fast and looked down; hands that didn't have anyone to hold them. They were strong hands now, and they had held the smaller hands of many.

The water was starting to get cold. I had been here so long, my fingers were wrinkling up like the soft hands of a baby unwilling to get out of the paddling pool on a hot summer's day. I remembered a passage from a book by Henri Nouwen that conveyed the deep knowledge that Ellyn and I had learned through our experiences of running.

Every time we make the decision to love someone, we open ourselves to great suffering, because those we most love cause us not only great joy but also great pain. The great-est pain comes from leaving. When the child leaves home, when the husband or wife leaves for a long period of time or for good, when the beloved friend departs to another country or dies . . . the pain of the leaving can tear us apart.

Still if we want to avoid the suffering of leaving, we will never experience the joy of loving. And love is stronger than fear, life stronger than death, hope stronger than despair. We have to trust that the risk of loving is always worth taking.[88]

I stepped out of the bathtub and allowed the soft terry towel to engulf me. I honored myself as I dried my body. I honored those who had gone before me. I honored the spirit of the women who wanted to run and yet stayed. I honored those who ran anyway and hid in cornfields, in closets, and under beds. I honored the teenage girls, not yet women, who made pledges to stay and commitments to be present in their own lives. It was a journey of discovery, and if we ran too fast, we would miss things. I had missed enough, I decided. I was going to walk, to see, to listen. I was going to stay, with myself, for a moment.

In a society that focuses on people's superficial characteristics, it is easy to forget the value and worth of the heart and the strength of the spirit. Throughout this book, we have talked about value and worth, and how the fact that they are often defined outwardly leads to conflicts in one's relationship with oneself and with others. Our true, intrinsic worth can never be measured or stolen by another or by outside sources. We may forget that we have that worth, but it is not gone.

For people who identify as "outsiders," this is an important

88. Henri J. M. Nouwen, *Can You Drink the Cup?* (Notre Dame, IN: Ave Maria Press, 1996). http://www.goodreads.com/quotes/492915-every-time-we-make-the-decision-to-love-someone-we

lesson to learn. For those of us who don't fit in because we have been defined as "troublemakers" or "renegades"; as "problem children" who have become "problem adults"; as scrappers just getting by as best we can—those of us who are real-life "survivors" of bullying, meanness, cruelty, and trauma—finding inner worth is a necessity, not a nicety.

Your heart is precious and full of possibility. You and all of your difficult lessons, mistakes, and challenges, and even your ugliness, are precious. Your heart may feel broken, shattered, frozen, or shrunken, but it is still fixable. All hearts, as long as they beat with a steady rhythm, can be salvaged and fixed. The heart is one of the hardest working muscles in the body, and it knows how to heal far better than the mind. We just have to give it the support and nurturing it needs. We just have to give it room to find its way to the required healing.

It has taken both of us a long time—even in our adult years—not to feel like little lost girls in the world. We have a sense of humor about this, but the little-girl voices are always present and often afraid. Betrayal in childhood, as we have mentioned, sets the stage for a host of compensatory behaviors, most of which are not productive, and many which severely wound our hearts. Early abandonment by those we love teaches us to abandon ourselves, though this self-abandonment is precisely what we must avoid. In our healing journey, we learn that despite all the outer cacophony and inner voices of self-hate and despair, we must remain true to our own precious hearts. Those negative voices quickly lead us down pathways that are very difficult to recover from, and although it is absolutely possible to recover, that journey is all the more arduous and risky. We must honor and care for our hearts even when we feel alone—perhaps especially when we feel alone. There are forces far greater than what we know beckoning to our courageous selves and one step toward courage opens a thousand new doors. We have a name and a place in this world.

We do, however, need tools. We need concepts and guides on which to depend when we "lose heart" or lose our way on the path. Both of us have books that we love dearly and carry with us as reminders and guides. We also have a few loyal friends whom we can trust to have our backs at even the most awful times. We have had to learn to be that kind of friend to others as well. However, it has not come easily or naturally—we have been the betrayers as well as the betrayed, and the lessons we have learned are hard won.

Of these lessons, we've created a short list of the ones that have helped us to remain most true to our hearts and to respect and value the hearts of others. The following are a few key components that must be in the forefront of creating compassion.

1. Take responsibility for your actions, behaviors, and emotions, but do not use shame or blame against yourself.

2. Do not blame others; do not condemn, criticize, or denigrate others.

3. Do not waste time in the land of hate and anger. Feel it, accept it when it comes, but allow it to pass through you, and move yourself onward.

4. Treat all others as you would like to be treated. Honor and respect all beings.

5. Find solace and guidance in spiritual teachings and in the strength of your soul. From Buddhism to Christianity to New Age works, find something that speaks to you and can help provide guidance.

These suggestions are nothing new. They are well-worn tenets of knowledge in the tracks of many religions and cultures, and for a good reason—they work if they are practiced diligently. Find what works for you, and make it habitual.

Ellyn wrote the last story of this chapter on a Southwest Airlines flight to St. Louis on December 31, 2012, on her way home to her mother's funeral. It was the last piece written for this book and is therefore symbolic, written on the last day of that year and against a backdrop of loss. It is a story about a man, a relationship valued, and the fear of love lost, not to be found again. But we do move on—we do love again—and every exit creates capacity for bigger love to arrive.

He left his coat in my closet. He hung it there last spring when the winds were chilly by the ocean but the weather in Napa was warm. He often wore it when he came to visit—standing on the balcony, smoking a cigarette, warm in his jacket—and then returned it to its hanger in the closet among my numerous articles of outerwear. I liked seeing his coat there, keeping time with my stuff.

Through the change of seasons, the coat stayed and was a reminder of his return. A relationship of distance can be a challenge and a burden, but it is also an adventure of sorts. A visit to look forward to, and those wonderful anticipatory moments before an awaited arrival, sometimes make it more fun than the experience of seeing a person daily.

Conflicts arose for him with the autumn winds, and he talked of leaving. His struggles left me bewildered and on edge. If he was going to leave me, then he should just go now, but he didn't. Each new time he came began to feel like the last. My old memories of betrayal and people without the spine to stay surfaced within me. I listened for tones in his speech, inflections in his voice messages, signs that he was actually staying or that he was going after all. Still, I was delighted by his visits and waited anxiously for his return. Each time after he left, I checked to see if he had taken his coat. Surely, if the coat was still there, then he would be back. . . . Right?

It was pouring rain the last night he came. I met him with an umbrella, and we walked the path above the sea and talked. I meant to send him on his way with his coat and not invite him in, but I gave in to his kisses and let him stay one last night. I told myself it was not over. It all seemed so normal: him in my bed, sleeping in spoons curled together, no signs of any departure. In the morning, we had coffee and said good-bye in the usual way. There was no talk of anyone going anywhere, and the morning good-bye kisses did not seem permanent. I thought of the coat but did not offer it, and he did not ask.

Weeks passed, and he did not call; he did not text. He disappeared from my life as if he were only a ghost spirit or a cloud of smoke. His coat still hung in my closet, apparently abandoned. But as long as it hung there, in my mind, there was hope of his coming back.

He was never a solid in my life, always more of a liquid—slipping into the cracks and crevices that were barren and drenching them with his expected but still surprising current, sometimes explosive and soaking like a waterfall, other times a steady trickle to a downpour and then back to a drizzling regularity. Sometimes in those last months, he became a gas—like the fog or the wind—and he was undecipherable, elusive, unknown in certain ways and difficult to predict. When I thought I could see, I was blinded. I could not believe that he was gone.

One morning, I awoke with such a pain in my chest that I felt as if my heart were shattering like crystal on a hard floor. I was so tired of this longing and this formulaic response to rejection and loss. Before heading out the door, I grabbed the coat from the closet. It was a response before thought—*grab the coat and any other reminder of him and mail it to him now! Be gone, be done, be finished with this segment of time, unending and looping back upon itself like an old* Twilight Zone *episode.*

I took it to the post office, bought a box, and left it and its beloved contents—the coat—behind. No more days of putting hands in its pockets, remembering; no more hugging a semblance of something that hung on a hanger as it had on his body; no more paying homage to the cloth fabric that had once held love.

I cried a lot that day and other days, too. It was refreshing and cleansing to my soul and heart.

The coat's departure was a symbol I created to ensure that my mind could understand that a time had passed and that I could not and would not accept love on those terms again. We need to create such symbols and rituals to mark our changes and our choices. When we feel as if someone has taken a choice from us, often we only think to react. But our better response is to wait and decide what our next choice for ourselves should be. What do we choose to mail away to the return address, and what do we choose to keep? What small and large memories stay tucked in our dresser drawers and jewelry boxes? The memories of time can never be taken by another.

The memories are ours to choose and ours to keep forever. If we want them to fade, they will do that, too. I still grieved him, though his preciousness would soon fade. As time as I knew it passed, I wouldn't remember his touch, his kiss, his gait, his smile. I wouldn't remember what it was to identify him from a distance, standing among other men but known to me by shadow and form. I had already forgotten his smell and the feel of his skin. These things happen, like the tide and the wind and the passage of time. We let salty tears fall from starry eyes of water and soul.

CHAPTER 15

SINGING THE BEAUTIFUL SONG

Out of the night that covers me,
Black as the Pit from pole to pole,
I thank whatever gods may be
For my unconquerable soul.[89]

Learning to sing has been one of the most amazing gifts of this journey. For many years, neither of us trusted our voice to carry a tune or say the "right words." But this is not the case today—we sing out loudly and happily, and our voices carry the sweet melodies of life quite nicely. We had to learn to sing our own songs and not the songs of others. We had to learn to trust the sound of our voices as they were carried through the air.

We were always the sirens. We have been calling out from the rocks since the days of our birth. We have not been heard. We have been forgotten, ignored, called the whore, called the bitch. We have been painted as monsters. We have been painted as seductresses. Out of pain, we have caused shipwrecks. Out of sorrow, we have caused destruction. But out of hope, we

---

89. William Ernest Henley, "Invictus," in *A Book of Verses* (New York: Scribner, 1893).

have found our way to being whole and strong. We reclaim that divine feminine spirit of the sea and embody her. She, in turn, holds us within her gigantic, wave-like arms. She knows the way home. All of our lives, we have known there is a sacred source that feeds our souls, but early on, we could not name it. Then we learned that this source has many names, and all are good and rooted in divine love. We now know from whence we came.

The following dream was told to Ellyn by a friend. It reminds us that there is magic all around us, and that our little, imperfect efforts to strive toward the light are good enough to get us to where we need to go.

She rarely remembered her dreams, so when she had one that she actually recalled, she found it unusual and entertaining. This particular dream made her laugh. She woke up rubbing her lower back and then her shoulders; they were hurting from some weight she had carried through the night. She felt for the feathers on her back and the place from which they had sprung, aching and tender to her touch.

"It hurts to grow wings," she whispered under her breath as she awoke. They were no longer there, just the memory of how it had hurt as they sprang forth from the skin like bulbs from the ground in the springtime, then grew and collected feathers, as real to her as her hands and feet. It was a memory between worlds now, and only an aching, phantom pain.

"I had wings once," she told me. "It was quite real, but only in a dream."

We carry vast knowledge within us, and sometimes we just have to gain access to it. If we pay attention to it, this knowledge helps us to become who we were meant to be. Our daydreams and our night dreams can assist us in that process. Ellyn tells the following story of when her daughter was young but showed wisdom far beyond her years.

When my daughter was a little girl, only five years old, while traveling through the Amish countryside of central Illinois, she asked me if I'd ever wondered if what we thought was real around us was only a dream, and whether maybe there was some other reality that we didn't notice. I chuckled and said that yes, I had thought of that, but not when I was only five years old.

As we continued to talk about dreams and thoughts and the nature of time, she seemed to fully grasp it all, but then it was gone and forgotten as we moved back into our day-to-day existence of learning to read and making peanut butter sandwiches.

Many times over the years, as I have walked through the land of bad choices, broken-heartedness, loneliness, and sinking hope, it has occurred to me that there *is* another reality—one far bigger than my limited experience and vision—that carries me through difficulty. It isn't a magic wand or an instant fix; instead, it's more of a steady hand to grab or a solid place on which to stand—even if only for a moment.

These glimpses of strength that we find within us, but that are also bigger than we are, give us an opportunity to connect with larger possibility. This strength is readily accessible to all of us, but seeing it requires us to face ourselves and all that keeps our hearts and minds stuck in patterns that no longer serve us. When we are five, it may be easier to see all the possibilities of life with more clarity and hope than when we are thirty, forty, fifty, or sixty; but at any age, change, growth, and possibility are all still there and possible, even under layers of pain and forced unconsciousness that keep us from fully feeling, and thus fully living.

Getting to the authentic self that feels life fully is not the path most people travel in our current world, but it is the path that leads to creating a different world, first internally and then outside oneself. It is a path whose reward lies in the traverse, for there is no destination point, only a continual unfolding, becoming more of a self and more of an "awake" person in the world. We begin to notice that we are not our troubles, our past, our depression or despair. We are more than our thoughts, heartaches, and perceptions.

We come to learn about this place, so much more profound than our perceived limits, through stillness and listening and identifying all the competing messages within us. If we are still long enough, and we develop a willingness to face all those competing voices that continually whisper discomfort and defeat into our ears, then we begin to identify another voice—one that is deeper, clearer, and more focused than what we are accustomed to hearing. This is the voice of stillness. It has its own language that brings with it a strength beyond human words.

It is in that learned strength that we find the ability to heal our hearts and minds.

Some come to stillness through what they call meditation, others through contemplative prayer, and even others through facing and naming their own dark places of the heart. However we arrive, we must get there if we are to heal ourselves thoroughly and begin to grow. Like a flower to the sunlight above, we push upward, taking in light and transforming all the places within us, acknowledged as well as unknown, and then we begin to make friends with those aspects of ourselves that have held us back and created problems. As Dawna Markova has said in her book *No Enemies Within*,[90] we bow to the demons of the mind, and in our bowing, those demons have no choice but to change.

In the following story, one woman tells of her metaphorical quest and the small and large steps she took as she moved forward.

"This is shit!" I said with more frustration than mere words can give credit to.

I was talking about the journey. I was walking through a dark valley and meeting many familiar demons along the way. I was tired, as many women have been tired, and I just wanted to get there.

She smiled. "You never really get there," she who was within me said. "Where is 'there,' anyway?" She pondered the question, maybe asking herself more than me.

90. Dawna Markova, *No Enemies Within* (Berkeley, CA: Conari Press, 1994).

I stopped and looked around. The valley was definitely dark—shadows loomed overhead—and the brush was thick under my feet. Fear, a common companion, curled around my feet. *He is rather warm*, I thought. I had lots of bags; maybe I could unload some of them. If I didn't have so much luggage, this journey might go a little more swiftly.

I pulled the bag off my back; it carried the most precious things. There were many other bags, though, too many to carry, yet I had dragged them for a very long time. I sat down on a small stump, both to rest and to revisit. Maybe I could go through my things here.

I heard the roar of the ocean not far from me. The night air was brisk, although I was warm. I opened a knapsack and began to examine the contents. Some artifacts were torn and ragged; it was a miracle they had survived the journey. The trauma was there, the wounds, the hunger. A large, hand-painted stone was covered in a handkerchief. An intricate design was etched into its surface, the portrait of a thousand scars. I touched my skin. My fingers ran up and down my body; the scars were familiar, the design the same. *I don't need to carry this*, I thought. I was comfortable in my skin now, willing to share these scars with others, no longer fearful people would recoil in disgust. I dug a small hole in the dirt and carefully placed the rock within it. It was not a source of my shame, nor was it a banner of victory. It just was.

There were other things in the bags that I could let go of: past relationships, not-quite-forgotten wounds. People I had loved and lost. People who had hurt me. I found a diary in the bottom of another suitcase. It was red, although quite faded now. I blew the dust off the surface. I remembered she had been my dearest friend at times. Her name was Cherie; she had been my voice. I was going to bring her with me.

As I opened the diary, a sudden gust of wind caused the pages to blow away, and they began to tear and disintegrate in the wind. I grasped for them as they flew by. "My voice!" I said aloud, before I realized it was not on paper but within me.

I gathered the rest of my things. My load was much lighter now, and I could continue on my journey. As I walked, I noticed that on the ground, thick with brambles, there were also tiny flowers in a rainbow of colors. They sang to me from where they were, quite satisfied with their existence. They were doing exactly what they had been created to do. I could hear the sound of the ocean, louder now, the song of a multitude of sirens serenading in unison. A large wall loomed before me, like a fortress. I realized I would have to climb it in order to reach the ocean. I didn't know if it was there to protect me or to keep me from my destiny. Since my load was lighter, I wondered if I was brave enough to scale the wall. I wanted to see the sirens for myself. Their voices sounded much sweeter than I had ever imagined, but I had heard the stories of the destruction they wrought, and I wondered if some terrible fate would befall me.

I looked down at Fear. He cowered at my feet. We had traveled far together, but he would not be able to scale this wall with me. I placed the remainder of my belongings in my pack and strapped it to my back. With the strength of a warrior, I grabbed hold of one of the many vines of ivy that clung to the wall. There were many windows along the way, and I peered into them, the way one does on a double-decker bus during a night in the city, looking for a glimpse into the complex lives of others. One room contained a feast, a table full of breads and meats and fruits, wines and delicacies I desired. I was hungry—I hadn't eaten in a while—but stopping to eat would keep me from my course. I remembered the fruit I had in my bag: a ripe peach I had found along the journey. I had picked it from a tree along the way and could smell its juices through its soft skin. I didn't need to stop, I decided; I wasn't that hungry.

I began to laugh. I didn't realize how far I had come. I might never get there, or I might be there already, because who was to say where *there* was? There would be many stops along the way, times to enjoy food with friends, walls to scale, Fear to lose. The journey was inspiring me; with every step I was becoming stronger. I could hear the words beginning to form in my mind. I had a song to sing, although the song would be on paper.

I continued to climb until I reached the top of the wall. I looked down, even though I was scared of heights. My stomach churned a little, and I laughed again at how far I had climbed.

Once we have tapped into our authentic selves and embarked upon our healing journeys, we are able to live fuller lives, rich with compassion and strength. We no longer have to walk the path of power as the outer culture defines it; we can walk the path of internal power, which is far greater than the power of this world. It is also the beginning of learning to love ourselves and understanding our true value and worth, which will shine in the outer world once we know that it lives deep within us. Be true to your soul; nourish and cherish it. Let it define you.

We know divine love is all around us, and as humans we can tap into this source whenever we want. We have also come to believe that sacred love can exist between people when each holds the soul of the other as a precious jewel.

The story of White Buffalo Woman is a story that teaches us of this hope. It helps us to understand our connections to one another and to the planet on which we live. White Buffalo Woman, a powerful spiritual being, appeared to the Lakota tribes in North America over one thousand years ago. She is said to have arrived in a time of great famine and to have brought spiritual teachings and ceremonies to the Lakota that taught them to follow the proper path while on Earth: to cherish the planet and its gifts, and to understand that one does not have to struggle to survive. This story still holds great relevance for all people today, especially for women learning to reclaim their own power-from-within and strong, divine spiritual guidance. The following story is one version of this legend.

White Buffalo Woman saw their faces on the horizon to the south of her. She came from the direction of true north and walked the flatlands of the prairie before her. The heat of the day rose off the ground in waves, giving her a slightly obscured and fuzzy view of the men walking toward her. She continued walking toward them, unafraid as an apparent maiden alone, her gait confident as a queen's and steady as a warrior's. She noticed the men noticing her but not recognizing her for her true self. One man was smiling; his eyes, filled with lust, lay upon her body, seeing nothing of her true nature. She sensed his eagerness to take what he wanted from her and never to think of the consequences of his actions on the woman before him. If she had been a mere mortal, she might have been threatened, but, being goddess, she was simply amused.

She beckoned him toward her, and as he approached, she enveloped him in her white buckskin decorated with feathers and porcupine quills. A cloud of dust emerged over them, and in seconds, the lustful man lay as dusty, broken bones at her feet. Snakes found him and created a home in his remaining skeleton.

The other man, much wiser, and more respectful of signs unknown and strange women before him, fell down on his knees before her. She instructed him to return to his village and tell his chief of her upcoming visit and the gifts she would bring to the people. He ran back to the village, and she continued her journey with gifts tucked into the bundle she carried on her back. The prairie winds blew her black hair behind her, exposing her proud face, with cheekbones high and eyes that knew all of men's shortcomings but that still believed some could come to know the divine spirit that dwells within both men and women, seeking recognition and honor. Tiring it was to wander the prairie, but she felt invigorated by the giving of gifts to create new life, and so she went to the village that day.

The chief, a wise counsel and distant seer, had felt the presence of someone holy coming toward the village. The winds had foretold her arrival, and he had prepared a holy lodge for her. As she entered the village, she felt the acknowledgment of her presence and the reverence of the people. She greeted the chief with her eyes and created an altar with her hands. In silence, she worked and then placed her bundle upon the altar, opening it with purpose. From the bundle she brought forth the sacred pipe and explained its significance. The pipe bound men and women together equally in a circle of love, and its smoke was a prayer to the grandfather mystery of time.

"With this pipe," she said, "you will walk as a living prayer." And after bestowing her gifts, she departed the village. In the distance, they thought they saw her on the horizon, changing from woman to calf and then to buffalo. Her gifts gave them sustenance and life. Her gifts reminded them of the sacredness in their prayers and the sacredness found in one another.

White Buffalo Woman knew, though, that there were many intricacies to the gifts she presented and that this dimension of some of them would not be seen for a very long time. For where men seek to obtain and take for themselves a woman without regard to her worth, there can be only despair. Sacred love is mutual and lacks domination or the desire to control. Sacred love honors both partners and can never be seized by force; it is brought forth only through mutual sacrifice and mutual respect. It is an honor to love with the body, the heart, and the spirit. This rare and deep love is a holy fire that burns between two people and is stronger than time. To dishonor another is to burn in the dust and become only bones on the ground—not in an act of vengeance by White Buffalo Woman, but as a consequence of uncaring and unconscious behavior. Let us strive for awareness. Let us honor and hold a place for the possibility of creating that love.

Living from that authentic place within our souls opens us up to all the wonderful possibilities of life. We can choose. We can choose life and all its challenges, and we do not have to be defeated by it. This does not mean that we escape hardship and trials, but it does mean that we have begun to understand that there is a universe within us to which we can turn. Within that vast, internal universe lie many resources for our journeys. We change our thinking gently. We break our unhelpful habits of mind slowly, but we break them just the same. We notice our places of discomfort and work with our pain. Even into the darker places of our mind, we can bring light. Even in our most challenging situations, we can bring patience and comfort to ourselves.

The next story is about a young woman whom Stacey was fortunate to know in a very meaningful way. It is also about how our minds change when we shed light and compassion on a difficult situation.

I shared my birthday with a young warrior woman, a gorgeous teen with a life that should have spread before her like a bountiful gift. She was turning eighteen to my forty-two. We were both wise beyond our years and had seen too much. She was in youth detention; I was in a detention of my own—a detention of heartache and loneliness, a detention of regret. We spent our Friday nights together, and tonight happened to be our birthday. The girls in the group were excited about it; I, however, was a little fearful. I wanted the girl to find peace and hope, yet I wasn't quite sure how to package that for her tonight.

Then she told me how. "For my birthday," she exclaimed, "I wish to hear you all smile."

"Hear us smile?" The group erupted in chatter. We were a little perplexed; maybe she meant "see"?

"When we have our minute of silence at the end, I will count down from three. Then we will all smile at once, and I promise we will hear it."

We looked around at each other. We had grown to trust each other during this time together. The young women had forged bonds and revealed secrets. They had fought and cried and encouraged. We, the "grown-up" women, had also learned to trust. We had grown to trust the art of showing up. The ability just to "be" together had become one of our greatest gifts. We had learned not to interrupt, learned to listen, to hear. We knew which of us would shed the first tear and spill the first expletive. We knew how to open ourselves just enough; then, carefully, as though wrapping the most precious present for the most perfect person, we knew how to close ourselves back up until next time.

She would be leaving tomorrow, transferring to county jail to await her trial. Today was her birthday, and she wanted to hear us smile. The journey with these girls and with ourselves had become part of our narrative—a counter-story of resilience, of finding our power and reclaiming our voice. Ellyn and I looked forward to this time more than they did, I often supposed. We learned from them truths that spanned the ages and that had changed us in the core of our being.

My divorce had brought up waves of hidden trauma that crashed upon the shores of rejection. The wounds, to me, felt fatal. I had suddenly found myself facing my fears and demons, and my own abandonment during infancy; there were times when, unable to breathe, I had to run to my car or to my room to sob. As my body choked on tears, I had no choice but merely to breathe.

And yet on Friday nights, I showed up. I taught and shared and listened. I threw my wisdom like a lifeline to young women who felt as if they were drowning. I loved each of them with the love of a mother, willed them to sense the love of the divine in my smile, my gaze, my words. I loved them with the love of my own mother, she who had abandoned me; I loved myself also with that same love.

"Ready," she said now, bubbling over in her chair with excitement.

When we had started the breathing exercises, it had been almost impossible to stay still and silent, and to be alone with our breath for a minute. It was as difficult for me as it was for them. Now we were comfortable, in our breath and in our skin. We had learned so much about ourselves, even in that silence, more than we had known before.

We sat up straight and closed our eyes. That had been hard for us at first, too. We hadn't trusted each other enough to close our eyes; we had all found a spot on the floor we would fixate on, trusting more in our peripheral vision than in our neighbors. There was often a new girl in group who didn't yet trust, who would giggle or shift uncomfortably in her seat, but today it was silent.

Our chests rose and fell in unison as we focused on our breath for a minute. We felt the hard ground beneath us and imagined the roots of life burrowing down to the center of the earth. We would not easily be moved. We surrendered to the relaxation of our bodies. We had learned early on that trying is the opposite of surrendering. When we ceased our efforts and stopped trying, then we were truly able to let go.

We breathed together in silence as the minute flew by. We enjoyed this place of peace now.

"Three," she whispered. "Two." I awakened from my relaxed state and remembered her birthday wish: *I wish to hear you all smile.* "One . . ."

We smiled, all at once, and we heard it! The sound of soft lips and moist mouths spreading open like the heavens filled the room. It sounded to me like nothing I had ever heard before. It sounded like the voice of angels, like the sound of a thousand babies laughing, like the sound of my pencil scribbling into my first diary words of love and desire. It sounded like fifteen sloppy smiles all shining their light at the same time. It sounded like love.

Then we began to laugh, all at once. We couldn't believe it had worked. The birthday girl had known it would, and she shrieked with pleasure and began to sing, "Happy birthday to me, happy birthday to me . . ."

I laughed so much I began to cry, tears of joy and beauty spilling over my eyelids onto my cheeks, leaving sparkling trails as they danced on my face.

"Let's do it again! Let's do it again!" the girls squealed.

We wiped our faces.

I thought of the Washington Irving quote: "There is a sacredness in tears. They are not the mark of weakness, but of power. They speak more eloquently than ten thousand tongues. They are the messengers of overwhelming grief, of deep contrition, and of unspeakable love."[91]

At that moment, at that time of deep connection, laughter, and delight, I realized I had received the best birthday present I could ever have imagined. It was a birthday I would never forget. Ellyn and I knew then that the stories of women and little girls must be told. They were not just our stories, or the stories of the girls we had met; they were the stories of ages, the stories yet to come, the stories we ourselves were, in fact, still writing in our own lives. They were stories of trauma and resilience, stories of myth and poetry, stories of the voice that would not be silenced and the voice that would be reclaimed—and, yes, most certainly stories of the songs yet to be sung.

We are fortunate to have survived. We have known girls and women along the way who were not so fortunate. Women and girls beaten, tortured, humiliated, killed by supposed lovers or husbands. Women threatened and afraid who ended up killing themselves instead of being killed. Besides the ones we have known, there are multitudes of other women, many nameless, their humanity stripped away by police stamps declaring No Human Involved, as in the cases of unnamed prostituting women killed in the line of duty. Other unnamed sisters have been killed by barbaric rapes that violated both body and soul;

---

91. Washington Irving, date unknown, https://www.goodreads.com/author/quotes/28525.Washington_Irving.

some have survived but passed on just the same, long before their actual death. These are the things that make us turn our gaze in horror and whisper prayers of redemption, prayers to a higher power that will hold and embrace these sisters and transform their pain. It is for these women that we write.

But there are lesser horrors, too, often unnoticed and minimized. Women among us who are belittled by the ones who are supposed to love them, who are verbally, emotionally, psychically beaten down and abused. Women who have stayed because they did not believe they deserved better, who were maybe long-ago victims of some kind of childhood abuse, mistreatment, bullying. These women become their own captors, too, even silently, as they smile through their days and go through the motions of what we might consider an ordinary life. There is so much unexpressed pain roaming around in the world of women, hidden by the pretense of hardness or the mask of a smile. And it is for these women that we write, too. We are all of these women and yet none, because each of our stories is unique.

We are also fortunate to have found each other and to have become friends. In our friendship, we have found strength to be honest with each other. Cautiously, and with great care, we have learned to guard each other's hearts as our own, giving nudges forward at times, and solace and a place to retreat to at other times. When someone is by your side and believes in you, then you have the possibility of overcoming many things. We should all be so lucky to have such people in our lives, but women do not often find one another in this way, and so we end up suffering alone.

The old ways no longer serve us, though, and suffering alone, although it is still an option, might not be the best course of action. Life will dole out rejection, pain, loss, misery, and lonely times for all of us, but our response is the key to our continued movement forward and to whether or not we choose to heal or perpetuate our suffering. The strength we find as we unite our voices with those of others who have experienced life in a similar manner helps us along the path. Those friendly voices will comfort, instruct, and heal us when we cannot find a voice within ourselves. Those voices will help us regain our own if we let them.

This path is never linear. It doesn't meet a destination point and know it has arrived. It moves like a spiral inward and outward and inward again, always moving, changing from one thing to another, as it grows. Like the patterns on the walls of ancient Newgrange,[92] never-ending twists and turns point the way of the journey—always more of a circle than a line.

We still want to run sometimes, though not in fear of things or people who scare us. We want to run toward life now, with the abandon of a woman running to meet her lover as he steps off a train. We want life to run toward us, too, to grab us and spin us around until we laugh so hard that we fall to the ground. Then we want to stumble dizzily into the arms of life as it kisses our foreheads with the love of a father, a mother, or a husband who will never leave.

This is our journey.

We find along the way what Adrienne Rich described as a "wild patience"[93] that sustains us each new day. We find a way of engaging the world that changes us, and thus we change the world.

---

92. South of Dundalk, County Louth, Ireland.
93. Adrienne Rich, *A Wild Patience Has Taken Me This Far: Poems 1978–1981* (New York: W. W. Norton & Co., 1981).

ACKNOWLEDGMENTS

Thank you to She Writes Press for taking a chance on us, and for giving first-time authors an opportunity to use their voices.

Thank you to Annie Tucker, our fabulous editor, who assisted us through this process. She told us early on that we had selected an "incredibly complicated style of writing" and an unusual genre, but she helped us traverse our way through many points of view. We greatly appreciate her.

We thank Georgia Hughes at New World Library for giving us that encouragement we so badly needed to move forward, and Dawna Markova for making the connection. It was beginners' luck for us, and very kind.

This book could not have happened without the inspiration of so many young women whom we have known throughout the years. We love you and thank you. We wish you all the very best in your lives.

We thank our families and the tribes from whence we came. Ellyn thanks Jill for her constant love and support. We especially thank our children, for their patience and their trust in us to mother them well. We hope we make you proud.

ABOUT THE AUTHORS

ELLYN BELL has worked as an organizational leader with at-risk youth and addressing violence against women and children for the entirety of her career. She is the former executive director of the California Alliance Against Domestic Violence and the SAGE Project in San Francisco, one of the first organizations to address human trafficking and sexual exploitation in the country. She is a co-founder of the Sexually Exploited Children and Teens Collaborative (SECT) in Sacramento and a two term elected member of the Sacramento City Unified School District Board of Education. She holds a Master's Degree in Religion, with an emphasis in theology. She obtained her social work license in the State of Iowa. She is a survivor of childhood sexual trauma and exploitation. Ellyn is also a yoga instructor and a trained dancer. She is mother to two wonderful people.

STACEY BELL was born and raised in the United Kingdom. After suffering abuse as a child, she immigrated to the US at the age of sixteen and became exposed to exploitation and other traumas. Today, Stacey serves young people as the Youth Development Director for an urban school district in Northern California. She is a co-founder of the Sexually Exploited Children and Teens Collaborative (SECT) in Sacramento. She has a Masters in Social Work and is in the process of completing her doctorate in International Multicultural Education with an emphasis in Human Rights Education. First and foremost, Stacey is a mother, both to her biological children, as well all the babies she has mothered, mentored and supported over the years.

SELECTED TITLES FROM SHE WRITES PRESS

She Writes Press is an independent publishing company founded to serve women writers everywhere. Visit us at www.shewritespress.com.

Say It Out Loud: Revealing and Healing the Scars of Sexual Abuse by Roberta Dolan. $16.95, 978-1-938314-99-5. An in-depth guide to healing the wounds caused by sexual abuse, written by a survivor who's lived the process firsthand.

Letting Go into Perfect Love: Discovering the Extraordinary After Abuse by Gwendolyn M. Plano. $16.95, 978-1-938314-74-2. After staying in an abusive marriage for twenty-five years, Gwen Plano finally broke free—and started down the long road toward healing.

The S-Word by Paolina Milana. $16.95, 978-1-63152-927-6. An insider's account of growing up with a schizophrenic mother, and the disastrous toll the illness—and her Sicilian Catholic family's code of secrecy—takes upon her young life.

Seeing Red: A Woman's Quest for Truth, Power, and the Sacred by Lone Morch. $16.95, 978-1-938314-12-4. One woman's journey over inner and outer mountains—a quest that takes her to the holy Mt. Kailas in Tibet, through a seven-year marriage, and into the arms of the fierce goddess Kali, where she discovers her powerful, feminine self.

Where Have I Been All My Life? A Journey Toward Love and Wholeness by Cheryl Rice. $16.95, 978-1-63152-917-7. Rice's universally relatable story of how her mother's sudden death launched her on a journey into the deepest parts of grief—and, ultimately, toward love and wholeness.

Journey of Memoir: The Three Stages of Memoir Writing by Linda Joy Myers. $22.95, 978-1-938314-26-1. A straightforward, highly effective workbook designed to help memoirists of every level get their story on the page.